Having endured a decade and a half of mental health torment, rather than dwell on the past the author wishes to look forward and see what can be achieved in his future. At present, separated, single and on universal credit, living in Cumbria, he wishes to give back to society and those that have forfeited so much already. He is planning to help those who still suffer from their mental health.

He still has to measure each and every day with the ongoing battle with chronic fatigue, cognitive difficulty and short-term memory loss. He will look to offer what he can when he can.

More mindful, empathic and gained emotional intelligence, the journey will never finish as it's the journey that allows growth.

D1663037

To my wife and son, Nicky and Charlie, who, as millions of families have witnessed before, have been the recipients of the consequences of conflict. I cannot change my past but I can move forward to make amends and hopefully shed some light on what happened and why.

This also goes out to all the serving military, veterans and Blue Light personnel who dare to walk towards unknown dangers and represent the best in human society in that precarious see-saw of life.

Simon Richardson

POPPY FIELDS, PRIME MINISTERS, POKER AND PTSD – A LIFE NO LESS ORDINARY

AUSTIN MACAULEY PUBLISHERS™

LONDON * CAMBRIDGE * NEW YORK * SHARJAH

A CIP catalogue record for this title is available from the British Library.

ISBN 9781398415874 (Paperback)
ISBN 9781398415881 (Hardback)
ISBN 9781398415904 (ePub e-book)
ISBN 9781398415898 (Audiobook)

www.austinmacauley.com

First Published 2023
Austin Macauley Publishers Ltd®
1 Canada Square
Canary Wharf
London
E14 5AA

Thanks go to Marc-Antoine Crocq, MD, Lous Crocq for their article 'From shell shock and war neurosis to Post Traumatic Stress Disorder: A history of psychotraumatology. Dialogues Clin Neurosis. 200 Mar: 2 (1):47.55. For allowing me to publish their work alongside my own.

This book would not have been possible without the dedication and patience of the Veterans Mental Health Complex Treatment Service (VMHCTS) who helped me out of my hole and banished those demons I had suffered with for so long. Thank you, Dr Sophia Collins, Perry Devlin and above all Dr Gemma Parry who allowed me to confront my trauma and process/lay to rest/accept and explain why, so well to me.

Dr Ghosh, who was the first to spot the spiral of destruction I inflicted upon myself. He started my recovery journey and it was he that set in motion the path I am now on today.

What's it All About?

I can honestly say that in my time in the RAF (Yes, a Crab), there are things that I have seen and done that money could not buy. You could be the richest person in the world and you wouldn't get near to some moments in my career that gave me those WOW feelings. Several times, my breath has been taken away by the sheer awe and magnitude of the occasion. How many people can say that about their jobs?

This book will recall several such amazing stories but also the true nature of warfare from my side of the fence. It will also look at the reality of constantly operating in the theatre of operations and the aftermath of the fighting close up. Becoming a casualty as you fight the mental demons, and the Black Mist that descends after seeing the traumas of warfare.

It will also share a few of those amazing moments that are the funny side of the military where you find yourself uncontrollably laughing with the best mates in the world.

For me, I have to take my hat off to the men and women of our Armed Forces that walk the ground the enemy holds. Those Royal Marines, Paras, the British Army, and the RAF who every day put that armour on, heavy pack and weapons in ridiculous heat and walked out of the relative safety of their compound (unless you were in Al Amarah DC and Sangin) and on to the street; who rode those vehicles with no vehicle armour in the early days and had to protect convoys, people and supplies.

Not knowing what was around the corner waiting, every step, every choke point, every wall, every newly disturbed piece of soil by a roadside, had the potential of changing lives. It churns my stomach thinking about the courage of such a daily feat.

In the rotary world, we thought we were relatively safe in helicopters, we came back with holes in the cabs and the rotor blades or not even a scratch, yet we witnessed bursts of gunfire so near you would swear they hit.

More often than not, the engineers would find the holes as you didn't even know you had been targeted. Some, on the other hand, did make it back but with huge holes as the RPGs had ripped into the aircraft or rotor blades but failed to detonate.

Some made it back but only after being rescued leaving their aircraft burning on the deck but they walked away. A few got hit but with luck on their side, they also walked away.

Some never saw home again and were repatriated with honours as they should have been.

I heard the typical firefight being described by a Para to one of our crewmen and how they saw it.

"For us, we have a slow build-up when we are heading towards the enemy, initial contact is made, the momentum builds and then we take the battle to the enemy. The action increases and the fight intensifies until the objective is complete. There then is a calm down period before a sweep up and then completion of the task."

He went on to say,

"With you guys it's instantaneous, you are fired upon, you retaliate and then the actions over as you depart the area, it's all too quick."

It has also been said that when flying in the cabin of a helicopter, the soldiers are not in control, they are a passenger and are not used to sitting and letting the fight pass them by, they want to be in control.

I wanted this book to have a meaning, not just something to hand down to my son when I become too addled to remember what happened (and that's already starting). I would like for people to understand the fun, adventure, adrenalin, pain and reality of time spent in the forces.

Most of it at the beginning is bullshit and bollocks but the foundation has to be laid. I want to cover some amazing stories but also the realism of the effects of trauma. If I could get one service person or veteran to read this and realise it is their time to put their hand up and ask for help, the book has done its job.

The stories are from my time either working on the VC10 transport aircraft which used to be at RAF Brize Norton or on the mighty Chinook helicopters from RAF Odiham and the odd Merlin Helicopter trip. It also covers my descent into PTSD and how it worked into my head and challenging the very fabric of my reality.

When looking for all of my flying logbooks, I found diaries I had written whilst deployed in Iraq and Afghanistan. I have found five diaries so far but I know there is one still missing. None of the diaries had ever been read since the writing of them, so that was a shock to the system reading them for the first time after so long.

Lastly, if you are fed up then just remember, if you can't laugh at yourself, others will. Put your hand up when you've fucked up, it will always come and bite you on the ass. If you don't like the situation it's yours to leave.

Speak up, don't shut up, you'll come to regret it. When you do say something make sure it adds value not the opposite. When you do complain, make sure it goes uphill rather than down. Lastly, the only person that's going to change you…is you!

Respect

Life throws up all sorts of wonderment, challenges, hurdles, pain, and happiness. In the military it is no different, it is just shared sometimes with a bigger family. This book will hopefully shed a light in all those areas with the desired intention of making people laugh (hopefully), understand the realities of some of the everyday occurrences we endured and, maybe, cause some fellow servicemen and women past and present out there to look at themselves and say it is time.

Time for what, you may ask.

Time to reflect, time to come to terms with and time to put your hand up and say, 'Actually, I do need help'. For far too long, we have endured the pain, the sleepless nights, nightmares, anger, frustration, feeling less worth than everybody else, being misunderstood or not being able to communicate that, feeling alone even in a relationship, those very dark days where that dark cloud visits and doesn't seem to leave, relying on drink, adrenaline, drugs to ease the day, every day.

We struggle with the fight every waking moment, it devours us, eats at our health and soul, we are forever turning to find the way out of the maze but hit a dead end. We shut away those scenes and terrible moments in time and continue to push aside those supposed weaknesses, stored away in a locker that never really shuts and occasionally spill some contents.

For some like me, those contents didn't just spill but exploded out after being locked away for so long. The locker was full to bursting, its doors flung wide and flooded the head that it became too much, so bad that it shuts you down. You're coping or believe you're coping but you are barely sewn together.

Every reminder tears and rips that fabric holding it in, until it inevitably spews out and engulfs your entire world. Others around you see but you deny and push them away; too proud to ask for help and knowing you can't let others down.

How do you cope, how do you hold everything together as it was, you play the fool, you joke but things change, you change, you don't want to but it is happening anyway. You go along with the first outburst, the rage, the aggression, the depression, the angst, deeper and deeper you fall until you hit the very bottom.

There are usually only two ways out, the dark side or climbing that ladder to eventually feel the heat of the sun on your face and that sea air hitting your lungs to remind you that you are still alive.

There has to be a hand or help, support and someone to have your back. There is but it relies on someone very important, that's you, you have to have the courage to put your hand up. You have to know that you need that help and you need to know that it's time to ask. You don't have to know what you want or even how to get it, you just have to ask.

We band of brothers and sisters that have trained so hard to get where we are, and still so resilient and determined to achieve and cope, we do ourselves an injustice sometimes because of it, but we wouldn't change it for the world. It defines us, it characterises us, it's a pair of glasses we look through to view the world, the people and the actions of others.

We use it as our standard, our counterbalance and our scale of justice. We are fierce, we are aggressive, we are caring and supportive, we lead, we follow, we produce and achieve far beyond that thought possible from ourselves.

There is another world and there is support, you would wonder at what is available and who wants to help. There are thousands of us now outside that would travel the country just to have a brew/wet/cuppa to ensure someone's safety, knowing they are alright.

Medical teams and specialist nurses, doctors and consultants who all understand the nature of the issue. The path can be long and will be upsetting, but it takes just one step. Don't put your effort into fighting with yourself, put that effort into fighting that dark cloud, that monster that claws at you. Turn around and say,

'Today I'm kicking your ass.'

2003 The Invasion of Iraq

I don't think most of us knew what to expect. We had a standard roulement on the Chinook Squadrons of Northern Ireland, Bosnia Herzegovina and the Falkland Islands along with exercises with mainly the British Army. The Royal Marines utilised their Commando Helicopter Force (CHF) of SeaKing helicopters out of RNAS Yeovilton but that was about to change.

Some Aircrew had completed Kosovo, early Balkan war (Yugoslavia) and the first Gulf War in 1990/91, some still, had been in the Falklands war in 1982, a rapid but dirty, gritty war that tested every person's metal to the full.

I was 14 turning 15 at the time of the Falklands war in 1982 and like kids in school, we would always get the daily rag to read up on the news from so far away. We would pour over the statistics of ships and aircraft, the fact that both the Paras and the Royal Marines were going.

The news at 6 pm showed the field artillery firing and the bombing of the Royal Naval ships in San Carlos Bay. It was quite upfront and you saw the wounded being lifted of the helicopters with blooded field bandages and limbs missing.

The Iranian hostage siege happened two years previously in 1980, and I watched that live on TV as it unfolded. There had been a multitude of extremist bombing and highjacks, murders at the Olympics, Beirut, Iran-Iraq war and so on. Yvonne Fletcher was also covered and so there has always been a sense that the Middle East was always going to be a flashpoint.

My first memory of TV was, I think, when I was three, maybe four, and I remember asking my parents what was going on with all the noise on TV, it was the Vietnam war on the news. There was always the occurrence of the IRA and their vendettas towards anybody, even their own.

Even with experiences in the Balkans, flying conditions in the Falklands and the pity aggression shown in certain areas of Northern Ireland, many of us couldn't prepare for Iraq, it was a bit of an unknown as a lot of us had never been to war.

What we could do was hone our flying skills, train on our survival knowledge and utilise every brief and flying minute with an overlay of tactics. A lot of people who wouldn't give the RAF Regiment a second glance, soon found themselves being the ones that listened to every word and asked every question and demanded to know how, what, where, as if their lives depended on it.

The Regiment was responsible for teaching us In the RAF, NBC drills and weapon handling. They should have paid attention the first time around. We would also deploy with full Nuclear, Biological, Chemical suits, and respirators as at the time we presumed, I say presumed as we were briefed by our bosses that Saddam Hussein had a huge stockpile of Weapons of Mass Destruction (WMDs), what a crock of shit that turned out to be.

On air-raids, I saw a couple of people so panicked they couldn't dress in their NBC kit and just gave up, sobbed, thinking it was all over. We were given malarial tablets, Anthrax jabs and Nerve Agent Pre-Treatment Sets tablets (NAPS), these caused I believe the majority of the lost weight after three weeks of the squits, we binned the malarial and the NAPS.

We were used to making out our wills but the extra kit brought it home a bit more. We were given gold coins to act as a barter if we went down in enemy territory and had silk maps in the back of our crew jackets for the escape and evade part.

We practised desert landings, day and then night and then underslung loads day and night. Luckily, a lot of crews had deployed on Exercise Saif Sareea in 2001 into Oman from onboard HMS Ocean on a desert operations exercise. I believe it was one of the most austere exercises I ever experienced even harder than artic training and as such taught us very well how to cope with desert operations.

As part of our build-up to operations we had to get to terms with the AR5 (means the Aircrew Respirator model 5). It was an NBC rubber hood with a large window at the front that fits over your entire head and was inflated by a filtrated air system.

It fitted under the standard flying helmet and once on was comfortable and not that much of a bother. What did happen was the pooling of sweat by your rubberneck seal that if you flew for a long time, would eventually reach your lower lip and you could dip your tongue into the salty tasting sweat.

18 Sqn was split into two for the invasion, with Chinooks, crews, engineers, Ops staff, safety equipment people (Squippers) and an all-important Army Ground Liaison Officer (GLO, more about him later) deployed on HMS Ark Royal for the transit and a separate land push which flew in from Ali Al Salem that I was on.

I believe one or several RAF Aircrew Officers on HMS Ark Royal sailing to the Gulf were quietly bollocked by the Navy's Officers Mess President for the huge amount of alcohol they consumed and the amount their bar bills were, surpassing the previous records by some margin, they were going to war after all.

With the sea-borne units attacking the south of the Al Faw peninsula with 40 Commando Royal Marines (40 Cdo RM), we on land in Ali Al-Salem were to follow on and act as an overlapping unit ahead of 40 Cdo at first light. We were to take 42 Cdo with vehicles into the Al Faw.

Over the preceding weeks leading up to the night before going over the border, we had practised day and night, attended briefs, stole wood and made benches, tried to stop the Army Air Corp nicking our stuff (unsuccessfully, they took every solar shower except one), listened to a two-day airspace brief from the Americans that told us what every level of airspace from ground level to 30,000 plus feet was being used for, where we could go (not much choice) and definitely where we couldn't go.

We had a corridor five miles wide and all the helicopter traffic would go through there and return to pick up the next load after a refuel.

I was tasked by the pilot planner for the land push to attend the pre-Operation Battle planning brief, it was full of three-letter abbreviations (TLAs) and stuff over my head but the Order of Battle made sense, and I added my two penneth when required about what the chinooks' capability was and could we lift such and such.

On the return journey to our campsite, we joined the back of an American convoy which had a turret-mounted grenade launcher (Mk 19). I was driving the land rover and noticed a vehicle driving very fast across the desert on an intercept course in our 2 o'clock about a km away.

We had no weapons and so closed up to the American vehicle in front. The American soldier waved us off and this vehicle looked like it was headed straight for us, I stayed behind the vehicle. To my amazement, the American Soldier turned the grenade launcher and I thought that there was going to be a bit of a fight.

Where he turned it, kind of upset me a bit as it was directed straight at our windscreen and he mouthed "back off". My foot might have come off the accelerator rather sharpish and we slowed allowing the gap to increase between us. The vehicle racing across the desert then joined the back of the American convoy and eventually, we parted company and headed on our merry way back to Ali Al-Salem.

There were some terrific storms during the lead up to the start of the campaign and one night our tent which housed 8 or 10 of us started to come apart. Boxer shorts and goggles were the order for the night and that sand was certainly a good exfoliator as we battled with the elements to mend the tent from the outside.

During our time at Ali Al-Salem, we often had visits from Saddam Hussein's Scud missiles. He certainly had a few in his collection to get rid of but we had the American Patriot missile defence system guarding our area and all the scuds I heard of or witnessed were intercepted by this system.

Most of the times, we couldn't do anything about these attacks as we were in the middle of the desert or had no hardened protection to get under. One such attack saw three crews being briefed by Officer Commanding 18 Sqn at the time Wing Commander Dave Prowse on the ramp of one of the Chinooks.

We heard a huge explosion above our heads as the Patriot missile hit its intended target. There was a huge cloud left from the explosion and we all thought about our NBC drills but as the cloud was swept away with the mid-height wind, we carried on the briefing. We did eventually get holes dug in and around the accommodation area, then ISO containers dug into the desert and eventually concrete shelters.

A good tale would be of myself and a Master Aircrew called Taff Bence or the Fluid Druid (Fluid because he has an immense ability to maintain the same drinking level of alcohol for ages and well passed any normal human consumption and Druid because he is Welsh).

If you go out on a bender with Taff and survive the next morning when you look and feel like shit, if you say I've been Benced then everyone will know what's happened. We had got hold of a Land Rover and went to visit an old mate of mine on the Tornado detachment line.

The Tornados had been stationed in Ali Al-Salem for some years to provide overwatch and to ensure Saddam Hussein's air force didn't fly in the designated no-fly zones. One was over northern Iraq to protect the Kurds, the other a southern zone was to protect the Shite population and the Marsh Arabs.

This friend (remains nameless as still serving but I will call him Tony W) could get hold of most things we didn't have. We were in a tented city with poor food but comfortable (I like most people out there at the time came back severely lighter than when we deployed. I was just over 12 ½ stone on deployment and returned less than 10 stone), these fast jet crews were living in a palace in comparison but hey, they had sorted themselves out over the years, why wouldn't you?

Arriving at the meeting place, we were greeted by Tony W and given a box of 24 ice creams, oh the luxury. Taff put them on the passenger seat when there was an almighty bang and the Air Raid sirens went off. Running into the nearest NBC shelter (Tornado Det), masking up with the respirator and then donning our NBC suits and boots.

We found out that the bang was the patriot going supersonic and the bang was in fact the sonic boom. I and Taff were sitting amongst the airman and women attached to or on the Tornado Sqn. We didn't want to get found out but how silly was that thinking about it now when you couldn't recognise anybody anyway.

Someone from our helicopter branch did ask for something from the fast jet boys but were firmly told to not darken their doorstep again, they didn't want to give up anything they had. Sitting there sweating away thinking of the demise of the ice creams on the front seat, we waited about twenty minutes to half an hour before the all-clear was given.

Taff and I ran straight out of the shelter, with a, "You have to do a sniff test first" following us as we ran to the wagon and back to our lines before they guessed who we were or worse what we had stolen.

We parked the wagon and sat around the front of the tent on our handmade table and benches merrily enjoying an ice cream when the rest of the flight returned from their shelter. Hot and sweaty, stinking of that charcoal lined suit and rubber respirator and most probably a little thirsty, a bunch of 18 Sqn turned the corner and saw myself and Taff enjoying a very pleasant ice cream, feet up, a bit nonchalant as if nothing had happened.

A bit of a surreal moment for them until the box of ice creams were placed on top of the table. They didn't last long and the word spread from tent to tent. Whoever the 22 others were who had that ice cream, I doubt there has been better.

19th March 2003 was our day to cross the border and go into Iraq. There was a bombing campaign leading up to that event and we staged forward in the desert that night after a day tasking. Let's just say none of us got much sleep and we were all up early for the move.

The Order of Battle for us as mentioned was to go in after 40 Cdo assaults from the ships but we had to wait for two things to happen first. The Americans wanted to use the airspace before us to move troops and the Ground-Based Air Defence (GBAD) systems of the Iraqi military had to be neutralised as much as possible before we went in.

As we found out, the Al Faw peninsula was well protected and had the Russian ZSU 23/4 radar and optically guided triple AAA batteries, some S60's, a single barrel AAA system and other pieces along with troops, heavy machine guns.

The Russian ZSU 23/4 is a formidable piece of equipment and to translate what 23/4 means is, the 23 is the calibre of the round and the 4 is the number of barrels that fire up to 4000 rounds a minute.

The Americans didn't muck about and deployed Cobra gunship helicopters and the almighty AC-130 gunship. AC-130 is a beast in the sky and flies faster than a helicopter, flies higher and has more accurate weaponry with a greater loiter time.

With its extremely accurate fire control system, the AC-130 can place 105mm, 40mm and 25mm munitions on target with the first-round accuracy.

We got the message we were to be delayed as an S60 was still operating near our landing site and it had to be taken out before we landed; it was and we were about to start up and head to the pickup point for our first serial.

Suddenly, everything was told to stop and hold, lots of questions were asked but nothing was passed to us initially. We then heard that an American CH46 with four American crew and eight Royal Marines on board had crashed and all had died. We then learned that an American Apache had also crashed.

The American air contingent we were informed was going to pull out and we had to sit on the ground while they did so. This caused a lot of disbelief as we were waiting to take in 42 Cdo, now we had to take everybody in, including what the Americans didn't.

I don't know the real reason for the Americans pulling out and don't want to speculate either but we had to wait over two hours and now it was bright daylight before we took off.

40 Cdo also wanted to know when we would overlap them as there was a series of manoeuvres and counter manoeuvres to take the British to Basra. What was happening was a large armoured military presence leaving Basra and heading 40 Cdo's way.

We eventually took off and picked up our first load, Royal Marines, a WIMIK land rover. Also coming along were two reporters and a cameraman, I remember one of the reporters being Jonathan Charles.

We also had to pass the CH46 crash site and look at the charred remains of the aircraft on the desert floor with only parts of the engines showing. I believe it was our second or third trip into Iraq and we had one of the Royal Marines on board and Dave Parry (my buddy crewman) put him on another harness so he could stand on the ramp and look at the crash site, his best man was one of the eight Royal Marines that perished in the crash.

We went over some water and the message from the cockpit as we were crossing the border and so we passed that along to the troops and made ready our aircraft machine guns. On our first landing, we put down and the WIMIK was driven down the ramp and out poured the Royals with the camera teams.

The WIMIK sank about ten metres away in the mud and Jonathan Charles ran out and started recording for the news. I was at the front looking out of the front door on the gun and looked at the Al Faw, a big comms tower, buildings, oil facilities and just to the right of the door a trench where only some moments ago, some Iraqi soldiers had been.

The prayer mats were still laid out as was the food but what surprised me was the pairs of army boots just sitting outside the trench. I think that while the army personnel can put on civilian clothing, army boots would surely give them away.

The Captain of the aircraft said we had loads to complete and we were still in a threat zone so Dave Parry mid report just dragged the cameraman and Jonathan Charles back on board.

We passed that crash site, I think, about fourteen times that day, it certainly brought it home that life could be quick to end. Three days later, two Sea King

Helicopters crashed into each other over the sea killing all on board both aircraft. I know this affected those onboard who had spent time and sailed with them from the UK.

We worked tirelessly throughout this first day as everybody did to get what was needed complete. Our intercom on our headsets was starting to fail with the dust and saliva and it was becoming difficult to hear the voice marshalling of the underslung loads.

We had an underslung Pinzgauer vehicle along with a 105-field artillery gun at the time when we approached the drop point. We saw a battery of six AS90 self-propelled guns and our track took us in front of their position. Metres away, we came to our senses and changed direction to take us around the back of the AS90s.

As we positioned the 105 and wagon, all the AS90s fired. The percussion shock wave moved the Chinook in the air as it pushed through the cab, it was quite impressive.

The shipborne Chinook crews, engineers, Ops staff and Safety equipment fitters (Squippers) all joined us on land a few days later and the Sqn was complete again.

During our time, we operated in and around Basra and Basra airfield supplying fuel for the tanks that took on the Iraqi 51st division. The Royal Scots Guards destroyed 14 Iraqi tanks in a battle and proved the Challenger was up to the job.

However, the old Russian T55 tanks that Iraq's had were not a great match. You have to consider the bravery of these tank crews knowing what they were coming up against. We dropped the Paras into the Basra area to take the town.

On the radio, we had UHF, VHF, HF and FM channels, we could all hear the air traffic and the fighter controllers utilise the US fighters that were being stacked in the airspace as fresh targets arrived to be neutralised. You would hear the call sign of the fighter acknowledge the details and then fly off to the target.

A few minutes later, the same call sign would call up the fighter controllers and confirm 'Winchester' a code word meaning all armament deployed and I have nothing left. The next fighter would then be called up and the process would start again.

We also helped move the Troops into Basra Palace to act as an HQ for the British Army. Basra Palace as the name suggests was Saddam Hussein's southern residence, very opulent and covered a huge area. It also backed onto the river which allowed Saddam to exit onto his yacht, this had been sunk a couple of days previously about half a mile up the river.

On one such occasion, we landed and stayed on the ground a bit, I think we were one of the first aircraft into Basra Palace. Dave Parry raced out and started playing with something by the front door. The Captain was a bit concerned and I kept waving at Dave to move his arse along.

On came Dave happy as Larry with what turned out to be Saddam Hussein's gold-plated front doorbell, he had only got his Leatherman out and unscrewed it from the wall of the palace. That doorbell now proudly sits or correctly is screwed to the front door of Dave's dad's house who resides in Anglesey.

We had trips we knew that were going to be spicy but when the boss comes up to the crews and says before you go and mentions that the sortie,

"Can afford to lose one Chinook full of troops on this mission and still be a success." That puts the trip into perspective.

Our Ground Liaison Officer was Captain Gareth Davies from the British Army embedded in our Sqn to aid in our understanding of how the British Army moved and fought (Order of Battle ORBAT).

He also provided us with intelligence briefs and what to expect in enemy capability. This guy was our inroad to the British Armies intelligence network and as such provided some good up to date information. He also had a foothold in the American Intelligence network as having the required security clearance which for us proved to be, most probably, life-saving.

The Chinooks were tasked to fly in a Para Battalion and take the Iraqi airfield called Qalat Sekar. The Para pathfinders would be taken in by two Chinook helicopters and recce the area. The two Chinooks would return and complete two other eight ship Chinook landings bringing in the rest of the battalion with vehicles, HMGs, mortars.

We were informed that the airfield was protected by a company size Iraqi Army unit about 120 soldiers with machine guns. This was going to be a big op and quite a tick in the box for both the Paras and us.

We had practised this before on the big exercises in the UK and usually had Hercules support with sometimes fast air. This trip was just the Chinooks. Twice the trip was binned for some reason but there grew an uncomfortable feeling about it. This airfield was by-passed by the American forces racing to Baghdad and as such mop-up operations of pockets of Iraqis were still required.

The GLO continued to utilise the American Intelligence centre for the latest information. A few hours before the Op was taking place he did a last check with the Americans and laid out the plan and route to and from the airfield. We are all grateful he did, even if the Paras are up for the task, there was no point in wasting life because of poor intelligence.

What the GLO found out was on route to the airfield was an Iraqi Roland radar-guided surface to air missile system. The Roland is a Franco-German built ground-based, short-range, air defence system (GBAD) which has a range of 8km and altitude of 5.5km. its rate of fire for the rockets was impressive and with a 9kg warhead could do some serious damage.

While we can defeat a lot of threats, this system could cause us a problem. At the airfield, the Americans informed our GLO that they by-passed the airfield as they didn't want to get 'Bogged down' in a fight as that would slow their progress to Baghdad.

What would 120 troops do to get you bogged down? 120, try a battalion of troops backed up with ZSU 23/4s and T55 battle tanks. This wasn't a small unit but a fully-equipped battalion strength unit with SAMs and armour. The story goes that if we did attempt to take the airfield and by some chance, we were not picked up by the Roland then we would have dropped off two cabs worth of Paras onto a heavily defended airfield.

They would have had to wait for over an hour until the next wave of eight cabs joined them. If, by some chance, the first Pathfinders cabs did get in unchallenged then the next wave of eight would have woken them up. While HMGs and mortars are effective, I think the balance would have shifted to the Iraqis on this one.

Three trips there, three trips back and a Roland hiding somewhere on the track, I also believe that not all aircraft would have returned home either.

There was the continual movement of troops and equipment around the area as new bases were set up and temporary, became permanent. We were tasked to take some specialist trips to an Iraqi airfield which had just been taken by American Special Forces.

We shut the cabs down and walked around looking at the newly deserted airfield and all the kit. There were lots of Armoured Personnel Carriers and anti-aircraft artillery dotted about with rounds still fed into the chambers ready to be fired.

We went into what looked like a garage type shed but made of brick. It was full of ammunition, all types and we opened great sardine type cans of 50 cal. There were mortar rounds and RPGs and most of it was Russian, it wasn't the writing that gave it away but the poor quality of the rounds.

You could shake the 50 cal cartridges and hear the cordite tip from top to bottom as the casing hadn't been completely filled. They might not have been the best quality but they could still kill you!

It was a definitive change in what we had completed before and a bit of a wake-up call to full-on war operations. What we didn't expect was to be there for so long or the disintegration of support from the Iraqis.

We didn't understand the political dynamics of Shia and Sunny Muslim differences or the influence that Iran would have in the area. The effect from Iran would come to haunt us later on, but for now, it was about finding Saddam Hussein and getting Iraq back on its feet.

I was very lucky in that the war had been declared over and with the death of my Grandmother in Scotland, I had a compassionate ticket home.

I arrived back late at night in Alton, Hampshire where I lived and woke early the next morning. Having nothing in the flat I ventured down the town, a five-minute walk away.

Very tanned but very skinny, I walked into a café and looked at the menu board. I didn't know what I wanted and when asked:

"Can I help you?" I said.

"I don't know what to have," having no choice for three months.

The lady told me to sit down and said she would get me something, she asked if I'd been away and I said I had.

"Have you been over there?" She asked and I said,

"I came back last night." I didn't pay for that breakfast and it choked me up a bit, I must say. After my breakfast, I completed a bit of shopping, not before buying a bunch of flowers and as walking, passed the bay window, popped them on the table and said:

"Thank you."

It was a surreal moment and as time passed and with more detachments to Iraq, it got more surreal, especially coming home. You would become completely enveloped in the day-to-day operations whilst deployed. One day you would be flying and get engaged by the enemy, the next you would be pushing your son in a pram up the road to the shops.

It took weeks to adjust and shake off the routine of Iraq and become accustomed to home life. We also brought home the smell of the desert in our clothes, kit and skin. You would sort out your kit and put it away for a few months.

On the build-up and packing stage before deploying again all the kit came out and still smelled the same even after washing it. It was a wretched stench that took you immediately back to the country. It's strange, while you could smell the odour on your kit and clothes back at home, it was indiscernible when away.

Alas, rather than secure and change the outlook of Iraq, it descended into violence and conflict between factions, religious groups, family feuds and those invisible fingers from Iran. We would become involved in so many other operations caused by these elements rather than build on the success of removing Saddam.

What we didn't know at the time and has taken years to come to light, was the fact, we went to war for a complete bollocks idea. All that trust and insurances from higher above proved to be a complete fabrication, we were all duped including those very high up in the military. Even now, we still don't know the truth or it has been hidden from us by red tape.

Don't Crash, I Only Need a Poo!

When You Need to Go
Make Sure You're Armed

One of the main operating bases outside of Basra for British troops was Al Amarah, about 45 minutes flying time north up the notorious Route Six. Having completed a week at Al Amarah with the tasking aircraft, we were due to return to Basra that morning. We didn't have any passengers or cargo and so it was an easy transit with just the four crew on the Chinook.

I was operating as the No1 Crewman at the rear of the cabin with the ramp M60. We had just started the aircraft power unit (APU) and I was positioned outside the aircraft watching the start when I felt that rumbling in my stomach and a bit further down in my abdomen.

I had that feeling of surprise you have when you know you have to find a toilet sharpish and your sphincter starts twitching and sweating.

The APU had shut itself down for some reason and I looked at the fault codes and informed the captain, it would be a delay of 10-15 minutes while engineers fixed it.

I informed the captain I needed to go to the toilet now, I came off the intercom and ran to the nearest loo. At the end of our helicopter landing pad plus a hundred and fifty metres was a single portaloo. I headed towards said loo at a rapid pace but not so fast I could become soiled.

About a hundred meters away, I heard a soldier on the path near main HQ shout "MINES" and I looked ahead and to the right and there was a pile of stones with paint sprayed on them. Sure enough a good indicator of a mine.

During pre-deployment training to the Balkans, we all had to complete lessons that could prove life-saving if caught in a hostile environment. One of those lessons was mine awareness, clearing a path through a minefield and marking mines.

Mines can be marked in several ways but what you look for, is man-made or a deliberate effort to indicate danger. You may not have a sign that says 'Mines beware', realistically you would use everyday items like an empty coke bottle on a stick with an arrow pointing in the direction of the mine.

Remember, most mines are found by the local populous, not the enemy. A good indicator is a pile of stones or a paint mark on the ground in a circle. Different areas use different signs so sometimes it can be a local thing. Point is, if it's mined, don't go off track. (We continue to be taught mines awareness every pre-deployment training course we attend).

I waved and jumped over the pile of stones missing the mine but really I wasn't that near to set it off by treading on it and burst into the portaloo. My world became dizzy, hot and sweaty for the next few minutes but after a while, I exited into the fresh air.

Walking back to the aircraft, I heard the APU start and kicked into a trot to catch up with the start. I did venture past the mine but kept my distance this time, those things have a habit of jumping up and exploding at waist height.

At the aircraft, I plugged back into the intercom and we completed the start sequence and took off towards Basra. We travelled at height to avoid the small arms threat and were over an unpopulated sandy/stony part of southern Iraq.

I was looking out of the port side bubble window (left hand) when my old friend, the stomach, started bubbling again. We were 20-25 minutes away from Basra, I thought I could hold on but I decided to inform the front end just in case.

"Do you want us to land Si?" They asked.

"No, I should be OK but thanks," I said and we laughed. Less than a minute later, that clench of my gut from top to the bottom, instant sweat and a sudden desire to find terra firma, I spoke up.

"Lads, we need to land, I'm going to shit myself."

The collective was dumped by the handling pilot, the power from the engines drained and we descended rapidly. We headed straight for a fairly flat shingle landing area. Bumping about as we landed, no dust landing technique, bang on the ground.

"Guys, I need a shit, I don't need to die from one, coming off intercom."

I said over the intercom and I unplugged my communications lead and for some reason, I grabbed my rifle and ammunition pouches and headed out the back of the still rotors turning Chinook. I wanted to get away from the blasting sand and I found a depression in the earth roughly 100 meters away, about 10 metres in diameter, like an upturned bowl.

I settled down as best I could with my combats around my ankles and sighed as the world exited my backside. During this event, I was looking around and looked up to see a huge hole on the other side of the bowl, it wasn't a hole really, I couldn't figure it out and then it hit me…it was a burrow.

Fuck me, that's massive I thought, twice the size of a badgers burrow, deep so it was dark as it fell from the opening. Wait a minute, what the hell dug that out, it must have massive teeth and claws I thought.

And then it dawned on me, what if it (whatever an imaginable monster from a land far away was, tusks, razor-sharp claws, poisonous spit) pokes its head out, what is it going to see? Some bloke shitting in its front garden that's what and it's not going to be happy.

Bollocks to that and within the next few seconds, I had loaded a magazine onto my rifle, made ready and was pointing my rifle at the burrow. Whatever was going to poke it's head out was going to get blasted by everything I had in the magazine.

So, there's me squatting with what seemed like a liquidised world firing out of one end while the other was holding a rifle at a burrow with an invisible monster waiting to rush me when I wiped my arse. How the hell was I going to explain my wastage of ammunition and get believed that I was firing at something that was going to eat me?

What I heard next was "Smile" and as I turned my head, I heard a click of a camera as Jonsey, the other Crewman on the Chinook took my picture, the git.

While I didn't require another emergency landing again that day, I do think we laughed the rest of the way back to Basra. That poor monster, fancy coming back home after a foraging trip to find that laying in your front garden!

The Continuation of Iraq 2003

After leaving in April 2003, I didn't expect to return in October but the roulement of Flights amongst the Squadrons had us at that time covering World Wide Operations. Returning this time to Basra at the airfield where a huge tented city had erupted and a weekly duty at Al Amarah with either the tasking cab or the Incident Response Team (IRT) cab.

The food had improved and we saw a full kitchen complement of military chefs churning out high protein, high carb food which was devoured rapidly by hungry mouths.

These chefs, in the summer months, had to work in extreme conditions, not only stuck in the tent but alongside ovens and steamers with temperatures reaching a ridiculous 60-70 degrees Celsius plus, inside.

The IRT cab was what it had always been, a Chinook with crew along with a nurse and medic onboard with a kit bag. We had a stretcher underneath the seats that was it. The MERT you may have seen on TV with the Doctor, Anaesthetist, Paramedic and Nurse didn't exist then and wouldn't for a few years until Operations began in Afghanistan in 2006.

We also didn't have Apaches as an escort and would often go out solo to complete missions, there was nothing unordinary about that, it was common practice. If it was deemed a high threat environment for a particular drop or mission, we would go as a two-ship with another Chinook or have the Army Lynx with their 50-cal browning heavy machine gun to assist us.

The atmosphere was changing and even though still early on from the war, you could tell that we weren't welcome by some anymore. The Shia populous was getting influenced by Iran and as a neighbour with Iraq, there was a very porous border.

We were sometimes tasked to patrol the border for smugglers as everything that could get stolen was. For instance, we were tasked to fly an American team up and down the main pylon route that transferred half the country's electricity to the south.

What the Americans wanted to do was pour 50 million dollars in aid into restoring power to the southern communities, very much heart and minds. It was quite a big project but the southern Iraqis, we were informed, were getting annoyed that they were still getting power cuts and it was high on the list for things to be done.

What would happen is months of preparation and planning would go into the building of these pylons and restoring the electricity to the south. Great, one night the entire south was illuminated where there was power available, the next darkness again.

At night, the locals would saw through three of the legs of the pylon, attach a rope between a pylon and truck and pull the pylon over. Once it hit the ground or the cables did, it shorted itself out, blacked out a considerable amount of Southern Iraq and then the locals went to work.

They would cut into the cables and steal the copper from inside and smuggle that across the border into Iran. It was a bit of a lawless time with the locals taking many advantages to making money and usually frustrating the system trying to help them.

With this continual stealing and smuggling, we would be tasked with troops on anti-smuggling operations near the border with Iran. The majority of equipment, copper and other valuable commodities we were informed was going across to Iran for selling.

I did get into a conversation with an Iraqi local at Al Amarah who taught English in the local school. He told us a bit of what it was like to live under Saddam Hussein's reign. He said at night, he slept with a pistol under his pillow for over 10 years.

You never knew when you would get that knock on the door and where asked to come for a chat with the police or military. If you returned from the questioning, you were inevitably badly beaten. He continued to tell us it was a fearful time when you could never relax and there were spies everywhere.

He told his son to never answer the door after dark. What he did mention was that the majority in the south were very happy that we had toppled Saddam Hussein's regime but allow them to get on with their lives and not stay too long.

Hindsight is all well and good and we could have done some things completely different but you react at the time to the ever-changing landscape of events. However, we were ill prepared in terms of forward-thinking for the long term, rather than proactive, it turned into a reactive campaign but much of that was brought about by the militias.

I believe, if there had been clear decision dates set out, then the populous would have known we would have left by a certain date. Also, banning the Baathist Party, those in charge of infrastructure and the heads of departments caused the disintegration of a working government and its sub facilities. It's easy for me to spout and realistically, I was a minnow in a sea of minnows just completing the necessary tasks to achieve the bigger picture.

One night we were tasked to complete some Eagle Vehicle Check Points or Eagle VCPs. These are a series of drop-offs and pick-ups of troops you carry on board to stop and search specific targets or close off routes.

Usually, a stick of troops is dropped further ahead of the intended target if they are travelling by vehicle, to act as a blocking party another stick would be placed behind the vehicle and. Stick on board for incidents.

Once communications had been established on board with the ground call signs, we are utilised as required. We are used like a hopscotch game, by picking up the troops and leaping ahead of the furthest in front.

We have had multiple groups on the ground at once and it is a fine balance between catching the target or achieving the aim and not spreading the assets to thin on the ground and too far away from each other and the airborne unit.

One such night at Al Amarah, we were tasked to carry out EVCPs near Camp Victoria area on the border with Iran. We were to stop and search anybody or vehicle we thought was smuggling to or from Iran especially looking out for weapons.

With a group of 12 soldiers, broken into a stick of 8, that was to deploy and 4 that stayed on the aircraft to act as a response team or a blocker to escaping targets, we set off. Dark and using Night Vision Goggles (NVGs) we flew a few miles from the border and started searching for potential routes and vehicles.

We had deployed the stick of 8 once already but found nothing on the Iraqi civilian. We flew on and came across a couple of vehicles that the stick commander wanted to investigate further. We set them down near the vehicles and the 8 disappeared into the night.

"Ramp up, clear above and behind 8 POB," was called and we were setting up for an overwatch of the troops. This allowed us to provide protection for them, have a greater view overhead and to see further afield of incoming dangers, it also allowed us to put guns on as we went around, it is called providing 'Mutual Support'.

On our downwind circuit, we were providing clock codes and descriptions to the front end on what was happening. I was on the right-hand door M60 and Sgt M (still serving) was on the ramp gun.

The Captain then informed us he was extending the downwind circuit to which both crewmen gave each other green nods on the goggles of WTF. The captain informed us that he wanted to extend downwind to utilise the opportunity to teach a relatively new pilot in the other seat some basic flying techniques. This was neither the time, nor the place, and I mentioned that we needed to provide support to the ground troops and had to be relatively near them.

The FM radio crackled into life and the ground call sign K10B (Kilo One Zero Bravo) informed us that they had found weapons in the vehicles and were moving towards a building. I confirmed, we had received the information, and pressed the captain to return to the overhead as weapons had been found. We continued on course and continued away from the troops.

The FM radio crackled again and the pitch of the voice said it all, K10B saw a few men with weapons come out of the front door of the house. Then, the house just spilled out men with weapons.

"Break right, Beak right," I'm calling into the intercom as all I hear is,

"Now, 30-degree angle of bank," as the aircraft continues to extend downwind and away from the troops.

"Break right will you,"

"What's all this noise Simon. What's going on?"

"The troops are in trouble, break right and get back to them."

We turned right and set off towards the house and the stick of 8 troops. Both myself and Mr M were ready on the M60s with the laser designators on and beading the armed men as we drew near.

The stick called for immediate pick-up and they were using section withdrawal techniques to maintain cover while getting out of dodge. We came up to the house and saw that the place was crawling with troops.

Troops were setting up a machine gun on the roof and firing points being taken up by troops on the ground and windows, behind walls and vehicles. We just kept beading them on our way past but it appeared they didn't have any night vision devices to hand, which was to our advantage. The thought has to turn to what would happen if there was a spark to ignite this powder keg, later.

We went past the house and between the two crewmen, we passed the info on which targets we were taking, who had the roof and top floor, who had ground and surrounds. We maintained that until only the ramp gun could keep the targets in its arc of fire.

Once we had landed on the road, the ramp came down and onboard rushed 8 heavy breathing, sweating men. We took off and headed back to Al Amarah, the stick commander was shouting at me,

"Where were we, where the fuck were we?"

To be honest, I don't know, the maps overlapped at this area and the navigation system called the TANS also had hissy fits at the border. Realistically, I believe we entered Iran by accident and this was, most probably, one of the first border crossing points in that territory.

We landed, shut down and the task was abandoned or completed some might say. The next morning the Captain went to the morning 'Heads of Sheds' brief and at the brief the question on whether or not an incursion into Iran did happen the previous night.

The reply was, the border is very fluid around there and has changed hands off and on over years, nobody controls that area. That was it, escaped from a severe bollocking and got out of dodge with everyone's tackle intact, well done Captain.

However, I and Sgt M did discuss what would have happened if someone had opened up or even if one round was fired. We were there to provide transport and protect the troops we had disgorged. We would have protected them; it would have meant taking as many out as we went past as we could but it would have happened.

Thinking back now, God we were lucky, the what if's spring to mind and the potential implications are staggering to think about, best not eh!

What was happening more frequently, was the rocket and mortar attacks against military positions, Basra Palace and the airfield were common targets.

The air raid sirens would go off and as a game, we would wait for the noise of the explosion and guess how far they were away from our accommodation. As time passed, the incoming projectiles were becoming more frequent and sometimes in larger salvos, so instead of having one rocket, you would be lucky and get three, four, five, etc.

They were usually 105-mm or 155-mm shells from the Iraqi stores that had been stolen and were being set up with a makeshift launch pad and remote or timer firing system. While the British Chinooks had left for Afghanistan in 2006, the mortar and rocket fire from the insurgents in Iraq in 2007 intensified so much it was every day and sometimes multiple attacks each with multiple salvos.

It was a horrendous time being near a British military installation. Tracer and small arms fire became nearly an everyday encounter somewhere in our Area of Responsibility (AoR), with us there was a sense that there was a lot of fighting going on around you but also internally with the local population.

We had completed some tasking during the day and were travelling back to Al Amarah from Basra at night, on NVGs and at height. What started as a small arms fight over a river, ended up as a full-scale heavy machine gun and RPG battle from both sides.

It was like sitting in the gods and watching a firework display from above. Tracer of red and green (Russians use green tracer a lot and sometimes in distinguishes between small arms and heavy calibre rounds but also the gap, firing rate and size of tracer tells you also.

With heavy-calibre rounds, the firing rate is slower so less tracer in the sky and the gap between each tracer is longer) were being exchanged across the river from several firing points and then the heavy calibre weapon would erupt for a few seconds and then the RPGs would reciprocate.

We passed this information onto the Dutch over the radio, who controlled the area and they told us it was tribal/family disputes being worked out.

Diary

14 Oct: Basra two explosions.

16 Oct: Basra Palace, Al Amarah and back tasking with Lynx Top Cover, small arms on the way back.

17 Oct: Basra, Al Amarah, Basra. Day tasking, night return, a lot of tracer. Two shot reps but missed by 100s metres.

21 Oct: Find of the Month as a tip-off sees nine SAM 7s found at a location less than a mile from Al Amarah. SAM (Surface to Air Missile) 7 is a first-generation Russian Infrared shoulder-launched missile. It can be classified in the MANPAD group (man-portable air defence) of systems.

It is aimed at the target through an optical sight and when the tone of the missile guidance system starts to be heard, it is telling the firer that the heat signature of the target has been picked up, then the trigger is pulled and it is launched. Being first generation it is quite a simple piece of equipment in so much that the target acquisition goes for the hottest target.

It is a close-range device so it only covers from 3.7 to 4.2 kms dependant on missile grade. It can climb to an altitude of up to 2300 metres or 7500 feet, travels at 500 m/s and has a large explosive warhead.

It is designed for low altitude aircraft but can accompany other self-defence equipment as it is easy to carry and hide. The find though was a good one and Int informed us there was still another fifty out there to be recovered. Three of the missiles had their batteries attached which means they were ready to fire in minutes.

18 Oct: Eagle VCPs north Basra with 2 Royal Tank Regiment (RTR), route 6, found a stolen vehicle with AK's (Kalashnikov) in.

21 Oct: Detainee taken to holding facility.

23 Oct: Dropped 60 KOSB (Kings Own Scottish Borderers) low level north of Basra due to triple AAA threat.

24 Oct: Picked up a young girl with the Italian medical team. Took girl to Baghdad to the American hospital. She was a daughter of a very high-level Iraqi but subsequently died in Baghdad.

Returned to Al Amarah and found out a couple of days later that the girls' death had gone to a parliamentary inquiry.

Al Amarah Chief of Police shot dead.

28/29 Oct: IED Basra, 1 dead, 4 injured.

30 Oct: 2 x Medivac straight to VC10 from Shaibah logs base.

Baghdad starting up with 32 incidents in one day. 2 x SAMs at 2 Russian aircraft. The airport shut for a short while.

2 Nov: American Chinook hit by SAM Baghdad, 13 dead, 20 injured.

4 Nov: EOD exploded two huge bombs that shake our building.

13 Nov: The camp was busy yesterday as a water tanker was driven into Al Nazera police HQ, the car behind was packed with explosives and kills 18 Italians and a lot more Iraqis.

Int reports lots of ground activity. 3 Improvised Explosive Devices (IEDs) in Basra. One detonates late, one reported by locals and one spotted by a patrol. It was a Claymore mine with a pager detonator.

15 Nov: Over to Tallil (Italian base in Iraq) with the Italians from Basra for them to say goodbye to their colleagues that died from the Vehicle Borne IED (VBIED).

2 x Black hawks helicopters down, one shot at and crashed into the other, all dead.

16 Nov: We were called out from Al Amarah to return to Basra that night as there was going to be a Deliberate Operation. Our job was to infill 70 + soldiers into an area in Basra to act as a sweep up team. An operation had already been successfully carried out.

On reaching Basra, Int was sketchy as were the details but it was a pickup and drop off by two Chinooks very late evening. We were reviewing the imaging given to us by another asset when the Wg Cdr comes into the planning room and interrupts us with,

"This is from the top, it's a hot landing site, small arms expected at least." With that news, our intrepid Ex-Royal Marine turned crewman (Billy Draper) returns with,

"Yeah, thanks very much for that."

No ground comms, no idea who is on the ground. The question was raised if it all starts into a firefight, which one is the enemy? We knew there were snipers laid up to pop off targets if they became a threat to us which was always good news to us.

We picked up our troops and headed towards a district in Basra, we approached from the east but were told to hold off and we flew away from the city and were held in a circuit. Twenty minutes later, we were called in and lead cab (I'm No2) goes in.

What we were landing on was a sports pitch, what we found out was it was very, very dusty. The cloud that went up with the first cab was huge and fine, with no wind it just stayed over the site.

No1 cab said it was a difficult landing with the position of the buildings and dust at night. We had to hold for another ten minutes before trying as the cloud would not disperse.

As we approached, we knew that we would brown out quicker than normal due to the size of the landing spot and the fine dust already in the air. We hit a set of domestic wires on the way in and landed.

There was no point in voice marshalling or even giving a height talk down as the dust cloud had already engulfed the front door. With skill and precision (and a bag full of luck), the pilots landed and we were told: "ramp clear".

The ramp came down, the troops ran out and into the dust storm we had created. It was that dusty I couldn't see the end of the M60 machine gun sticking out of the door. There was no "clear above and behind" just a lift high and then depart once out of the cloud at a few hundred feet.

We returned to Basra and then back to Al Amarah where we continued to act as the tasking cab. When we returned, the Basra after our week away I talked to Billy Draper, who was on the other Chinook about the Op.

He asked how we got on and did we open fire? A bit of a confused look appeared and I asked why. Billy said that as soon as your troops came off the back of the cab, there was a massive firefight and tracer was going everywhere.

I had to be honest and say we couldn't see the end of the barrel, let alone the firefight. According to Billy, it was quite a good one. Ignorance is bliss and nobody got hurt.

We were to leave after our second detachment to Iraq but intelligence pointed at things getting worse. There were now several IEDs and shootings every day and RPG attacks for helicopters.

However, the last piece of feedback from the locals was that the majority still prefer the British as they have more freedom with us in control. The local religious clerics were of a different view and were ranting about death after Ramadan.

Continuation of Iraq 2004

We travelled back to Iraq for the Christmas detachment in 2004 operating again around the Basra area and further north in Al Amarah. The frustration from certain elements of the Iraqi people was very evident and expecting to be targeted this detachment as the increase in fighting between factions and the allied military presence intensifies.

One of our first trips into theatre was to the Japanese camp call sign Asamoa or 'Grey 104' in our Helicopter Landing Site Directory (HLS). We had just dropped off troops at Grey 101 when the only remaining passenger, an army Captain said he wanted to go to Grey 104.

We found the site not too far away from the last drop. Looking through the HLS Directory for the area, we found the Landing Site (LS) picture in the book. Having looked at the camp and direction of the HLS, we found the big painted 'H' on the ground.

Pre-landing checks all good and we proceeded to position to land. Coming in, we noticed some tents nearby that really shouldn't be near the site, they started blowing and so we moved away and landed near. The Army Captain exited the ramp and we took off.

Returning to Grey 101, we were informed that we had dropped the Captain at the wrong site. The conversation bounced back and forth that the captain was sure he wanted Grey 104.

"Well, he doesn't want to stay there anymore and can you pick him up but not at the same site you just went to."

We returned, flew a complete recce around and over the site. We found a new 'H' and descended to pick up our lost Captain. On he came followed by two cross looking Japanese soldiers, one of which spoke very good English, the other officer was rather angry.

Over the din of the helicopter running, I could make out that they were very angry about the landing at the old LS. I showed the HLS directory to the Japanese soldier and explained as best as I could that the HLS directory shows the old site. He then offered a delightful gift of a large bag of Japanese savoury snacks, bowed and left. That was the politest bollocking I had ever received.

On return to Basra, there may have been a little bit of a dispute over our actions. While the Japanese were there as none armed humanitarian mission, they did have some very Gucci kit. Unfortunately that Gucci kit was in the tents that were blown by our downwash.

The Japanese had four helicopter UAV's in theatre, we had just trashed two. Remember, this was 2004 and who had heard of a helicopter UAV? It was estimated that we had caused 50,000 dollars' worth of damage.

Back at the Basra, the finger-pointing started and we were put under the spotlight about our actions. We landed in the correct location, the HLS directory was up to date (changed every six months), the new LS was at an entirely different location surrounded by ISO containers so not visible unless flying over the top.

The Japanese had moved their HLS for whatever reason, which is entirely up to them, but had unfortunately not passed the detail onto the Mobile Air Operations Team (MAOT) who recce the sites and built the HLS directory. I think we apologised but called it a draw.

On the return journey, we had to pick up a load of Czech nurses from Shaibah logs base. That may have been the sweetest smelling trip in my entire time in theatre.

Christmas week was spent at Al Amarah and we tasked twice on Christmas Day with EVCPs. Instead of the British Army in the back, we had the Iraqi Army. We gathered them up but there was a slight smell of alcohol, whether Dutch courage for the trip or an excuse to celebrate Christmas even though they were Muslim, I don't know.

Our first trip saw the Iraqis complete two serials of EVCPs before they wanted to return to Al Amarah after about an hour. The second trip was worse with six of the soldiers being sick over each other as they had consumed more alcohol and we binned the trip off as they were unfit for the task.

Post-Christmas and before the new year we had a lot of tasking to recce sites and roads leading to Al Majar Al Kabir. We were informed that British troops would be entering the town in the next few days.

We searched the routes in to find potential roadside bombs and to report back findings and new ground movement i.e. digging, the build-up of containers, oil drums, etc, newly placed by the roadside. There was one IED identified on the route out of Al Amarah which EOD dealt with.

Al Majar Al Kabir was the scene of fighting the previous year in 2003 which saw a Para patrol come under attack and six RMP's who mentoring the local police, were murdered with their weapons by a 600 strong crowd.

The town had not been entered for six months by the British but with diplomacy, there was an opportunity to allow the local police and Iraqi National Guard back into the town to take control and provide assistance in rebuilding amenities and infrastructure.

Personally, I had a bone to pick with these people. Highly unprofessional I know, and I would undoubtedly get into trouble if anything had happened, but I wanted it to kick off. My girlfriend was attached to the army medical unit even though with the RAF over that period in 2003.

She not only had to collect the six murdered RMP's with other medical staff, but she had also to deal with the injured flown in by Chinook that had been shot up over the town which had several casualties on board also.

While medically trained, nothing prepares you for the scenes in the police station and as such, she lost the majority of her hair the following year. Good news though as she grew it all back before we married in 2004. Communications were not great between the Chinook and the Field Hospital after the shoot up and even though the message was passed to the ground comms unit, it didn't reach the hospital.

The first they knew was a chinook landing right next to the hospital tents and then all hell broke loose. My wife looked after the soldier with the gunshot wound to the head that had been sitting on the Crewman seat at the front. Unfortunately, the only British anaesthetist in theatre, I believe, was on the Chinook that took the rounds and had a foot wound from one of them.

Eight soft top snatch land rovers were going to enter the town Al Majar Al Kabir with a Colonel taking the meeting with the elders and town leaders. This wasn't a good place for the British and the Int was that it could turn nasty anytime. There had to be a show of force as like previously the odds could be overwhelming.

We were tasked for overwatch and if it turned nasty to target the leakers (main insurgents) who may have tried to escape from the town. We had Intelligence on who they were and where they would run from and direction they would bug out to.

On route six, the main highway north there were at least 20 Warrior armoured personnel carriers (APCs) and 4 Challenger main battle tanks. There are always spotters out gathering information (we call them Dickers) and it would have been noted that the massing of a collection of tanks, armoured vehicles and soldiers were only a couple of kms away.

I believe that Colonel also mentioned that if anything happened to his troops at this meeting, then the town would feel the weight of the British Army. Whether or not that kind of message was passed to the locals, I am sure they knew exactly what would happen if they started a firefight.

The meeting passed and the Colonel with entourage got into their vehicles. Boys could be seen trying to break anything off the vehicles as they started to move and then the stone-throwing erupted but on the whole, it had worked. The message was passed to the townsfolk, only one soldier was injured and everybody made it back to base.

One of the strangest tasking orders to come down to us in January was a munitions move. Once we found out what exactly was on the books, we firmly turned that off. We were being asked to assist in moving some Iraqi munitions, this seemed a bit odd as we regularly move ammunition around the theatre.

Then we were informed that we had to take our respirators on the trip just in case, WTF are we supposed to be carrying, I think was the question raised? A large store of ammunition had been found but EOD was unsure what exactly the shells were.

As we found out, the shells weren't in any packaging that would identify them and had no markings. The army didn't want to take the shells on a four-tonner military vehicle due to the risks of carrying that kind of ordinance on a bumpy road.

Through the expletives we gave to the boss I think he got the point that shells are hard to restrain on a helicopter and with all the vibration and turning, they would easily move around the cab.

What about putting all the shells into a net and underslung it then? So picking up a net of shells that will tumble around the net is going to help who, especially with all those holes in it? I think all the crews were in agreement that this was a silly idea. We had no idea what state they were in, the decay or how safe they were.

We didn't even know what was inside but it gave the army jitters enough to bang the task to us. What started as the army plan to follow us in a couple of four-ton trucks at a very safe distance with the shells inside the helicopter, turned to us following them at a safe distance with the munitions in their truck.

We put a case in, saying that if one of the shells went off, the Chinook would disintegrate but if it went off in the army truck, we could be the medical cover to get them to hospital. What they thought may have been in them was Mustard gas but who knows now, the entire stores were buried in a huge pit in the middle of the desert.

The nasty side of IEDs or homemade bombs were becoming commonplace and more sophisticated ways of detonation were being practised. This didn't come from the Iraqi army; these were new skills being taught to the insurgents by a menacing neighbour.

We were tasked many times for recce duties and the idea was to fly a route and check out for hazards. On 30 January 2005, we were tasked to complete a recce near MAK (not sure the designation of MAK now). We found five new piles of stones that would have been big enough to hide 155mm shells or act as makers.

The idea is that as the vehicle passes the large marker the person detonating would see that the vehicle was in the correct location to cause the most damage and either by remote or command wire, detonate the explosives.

This means the person detonating the device was within a few hundred metres, maybe a km away with binoculars. This was reported back and we went to bed. That night we were mortared with one blind and one going over the top but still missing.

Luckily, the rains had made any soil/sand/desert into a bit of a quagmire and as such if you stepped in it, you would end up caked in the stuff, it was that gloopy. It helped us one evening as one of the four crew persons at Al Amarah, we were returning from the evening meal at about 18:45.

We were talking on route to our accommodation near the flight line when we heard a plop, in the distance, like a soft slapping of clay. Then we heard a soldier shout,

"What are you lot doing, get under cover, we're being mortared?" Another plop and then we ran, but someone started to giggle and then all started to giggle and then laugh.

By the time we were by the door to the accommodation, we were all breathless but still laughing. One of those moments, when inexplicably, you find the funny side even when it's dangerous.

A good day for us at work would be the EVCPs and finding something of value, no, not a gold-plated doorbell. We dropped a stick of troops to search areas and they came across a stash of over one hundred 155 mm shells. These artillery pieces were being used now as IEDs along routes and being fired from makeshift platforms at us.

This was a major find and great news that these had been taken off the radar of the insurgents. Another recce trip before the EOD was to travel to the east to blow up old shells and napalm. We spotted several 155 mm shells on the route and the EOD was tasked to investigate, another good spot.

20 Jan 2005 saw us completing several troops trips from Shaibah Logistics Base returning to Basra for the troops R&R break halfway through their tour. It was only a five-minute journey to and from the airfield and we had completed several serials and were returning to Shaibah when I saw an explosion in our 2 o'clock.

The cab was in a left hand turn for the LS, so eyes were out for that at the front and I called "explosion right 2 o'clock, 300 metres."

There was a reply from the front that it was most probably EOD getting rid of ammunition finds, which made sense. We carried on tasking and the next two serials were just odd. Before, the troops were happy that they were going home for a week or so, really up for it.

The last two, especially the last one was filled with a few jittery, nervous people. We completed the task and shut down and went to Ops to compete the debrief. We found out then that it wasn't EOD blowing up stuff but a Vehicle Borne Improvised Explosive Device (VBIED) at the main gate of Shaibah logs base.

Two Iraqi's dead, several locals injured along with four British troops. The insurgents had kidnapped a local man's wife and children and tasked him with driving the vehicle to the main gate or all his family would be killed. He had no choice but the Insurgents detonated the bomb with him inside.

We did ask the question of why were we not told over the radio, not because of the risk but because we were a huge asset on site with the means to use as a recce or troop mover or even casualties. To be fair to them as the Crewman Leader said, we wouldn't have made a difference as it would have been bedlam for the first half an hour.

It was definitely hotting up in the sense of attacks against the Multi-National Force and the first free elections in Iraq were due to take place on 30 January

2005. There was a lot of Iraqi security and police out and Basra had a curfew at night to stop the insurgents from setting up IEDs and revenge killings. There was also a lot of attacks against multi-national forces up North in and around Baghdad and against aircraft.

Diary between 21 January 2005-7 February 2005

21 Jan: Italian Heli attacked with small arms and heavy machine gun (SA/HMG). 1 dead crewman, 1 injured. SeaKing helicopter 845 Sqn small arms fire (SAFIRE) contact.

27 Jan: SAFIRE against Lynx. Potential suicide bombers coming south from Baghdad. Road convoy attacked with SA. 3 days to the Iraqi elections.

28 Jan: US 53 hello goes down killing 31 onboard + 6 extra deaths up north. The Yanks had 38 separate attacks on them today. They are taking a hell of a kicking.

29 Jan: Curfew imposed in Basra, checkpoints set up on every major road.

30 Jan: People generally happy to be allowed to vote. News in, a British Hercules aircraft has crashed NW of Baghdad. No numbers yet.

31 Jan: Large explosions in Basra.

2 Feb: Over 200 attacks on multi-national forces, coalition, Iraqi National Guard and Iraqi Police Service and civilians today. Several killed.

7 Feb: Repatriation ceremony for the 11 British service personnel from the Hercules crash in Baghdad. Paid respects at 16:00 and thousands on parade from all nations as the 11 Union flag draped coffins were blessed and transported on to the back of a Hercules for the return trip to the UK.

This was also the detachment where my mate and opposite number Mac MacKenzie had that terrible trip outside the airborne Chinook (See Basra moment).

One of the hardest things to cope with, is the kids that get hurt. There were a few in Iraq and not all we could save. We got an IRT shout to go pick up two boys who had been found after an explosion. They had found an ammunition store and broken in to get the copper banding of the shells.

It appears that they got a bit heavy handed while trying to knock the copper bands off and one exploded. These boys had lost both their arms in the blast and other injuries. Before we even took off, the task was turned off. The reason I heard, whether true or not was that we were there for military matters not as an Iraqi ambulance service.

After completing four detachments to Iraq, I was then tasked to deploy to Afghanistan in Feb 2006 to Kandahar. The British army stayed in Iraq for far too long and the Merlin fleet took over from where we were at Basra.

Unknown at the Time My Most Professional Flight

During the winter months leading up to Christmas 2004, Iraq had become a bit of a quagmire. Heavy rain flooded parts of the south and made a very muddy/clay top layer. The pollution from the brick factories clung in the air, you knew when you were near the brick factories when you sucked in that acrid smoke that swept through the cab and clung to your combats.

As a crew of four with a pilot, Nav and two crewmen, we had been crewed together for quite a few weeks on the Chinook. Our tasking ranged from normal resupply activity whether internal cargo, trooping or underslung load (USL) or sometimes all three at once.

Attacks and Raids (now called Deliberate Ops) and the casualty evacuation (Casevac) aircraft deployed to areas to provide that golden hour transport to a hospital for the injured. It was called the IRT cab or Incident Response Team.

We had briefed for the nights' sortie and had an update on hostile activity and general intelligence of Basra at Operations (Ops). We were to complete a round-robin effect to transport mainly troops to and from Shaibah Logistics base, Basra Palace (British Forces HQ in Basra), The Shatal Arab base and Basra Airfield. Just think of it as a bus journey but with guns and working on night vision goggles, quite routine and a familiar pattern.

We completed several serials in the dark but it was getting darker and the millilux light levels had dropped well below 10. If I am honest it was pitch black off goggles but enough light from the city to make it work. We were on our last run into Basra Palace and we approached away from the city from the south or east as the Palace was on the South East side of the City.

We usually crossed close to the river that sometimes marked the border between Iraq and Iran. You would know you were close to Iran as the Chinooks Radar Warning Receiver (RWR) would pick up the radar signatures (called 'being painted') of Iran's integrated air defence system or IADS. the Russian made SA6 or the SA8 (this was early 2000's) radar-guided ground to air missile systems would be indicated but others popped up now and again.

When Chinook helicopters pick up troops, it's usually done with the tail end pointing at the troops since the access is through the ramp. There are occasions troops exit and enter via other means by fast roping, parachuting or winching but not the general day to day tasking aircraft.

During day time, with the effect of downwash from the rotor heads, uneven ground and 700 degrees of heat being pushed out of the engines, whilst troops are carrying heavy loads, it is hard work.

Now add sand, snow, mountain ridges, a confined area where obstructions are very close to the aircraft or even at sea and you start to understand the complexities of keeping a 20-tonne helicopter where you want it.

At night time, it is even more important as you lose so many visual references that you scan all the time to ensure you stay in the correct position. The three things I learned about night flying from my instructors were, scan, scan and scan.

When you have night vision goggles, you have an advantage as the world turns green but is a lot more visible. Having what looks like two green toilet rolls stuck on the front of your flying helmet is extremely useful but it does reduce your peripheral vision from 180 degrees to 40, that's where the scan comes in.

Coming over the river, the pilot informed us that he wanted to land facing the troops. We hadn't done this for the previous sorties and questioned why. He wanted to do this and we had to follow his orders. We crossed the blast wall and descended onto the landing site (LS) with the cockpit facing the troops.

We already had a mix of British, Canadian and Americans on board from a previous pick up. As soon as we landed, the troops started walking towards the aircraft. We noticed that they were heads down protecting their faces from the downwash and blast from and grit/sand that was being blown up by the rotors.

This was bad as they were walking directly towards the front disc of the aircraft. At certain angles, the forward rotor head blades can dip to four foot four inches or 132 cm above the ground.

Just think of a thirty-foot blade, weighing 354 lbs being spun 215 revolutions a minute and then times that by three for the front rotor head. I don't know that many, if any, soldiers with Kevlar helmet and backpack/Burgan that can safely walk under that disc height.

Torches came out, yelling, the flash of aircraft lights but still this soldier carried on. Mr Mac was on the ramp leaning out, I was waving my arms and night light from the right-hand door and then the Captain called lifting...

Up we shot like a cork out of a shaken bottle of fizz. The captain didn't like the situation and took action. I called "height is good," as we were still Climbing and we stopped 100-150 feet above the LS. It was pitch black, we were over the British HQ which had most of its lights out due to mortar attacks and we were in the hover. Some seconds passed and the question was,

"Is everybody alright?"

We had to get our bearings and figure what to do now, realistically, it would have been a go around and do it again, but something wasn't right.

The pilot and Nav were ok and so was I, but there was something odd about the back of the aircraft that made my stomach turn, that gut feeling, initially, you don't know why, and it took a few seconds.

"Mac, are you ok at the back?" I asked over the intercom, no answer. Then it dawned on me, the ramp was still down, it hadn't been returned to its up position for sitting with the ramp M60 machine gun.

"Guys, I don't think Mac is on the aircraft, can you see him on the LS," I asked?

At that moment, Basra's noise complaint society decided to unleash about a 20-30 tracer burst to the front and above our position. Considering the gap between tracer, that's a 100-150 round burst.

The front end were looking for Mac the same as me but we couldn't see anybody near the LS. The Captain wanted to go around but I said we hadn't found out where Mac was. This was all going on in a flash and I got that very uncomfortable impression that Mac had fallen out of the aircraft when we lifted.

"We've got to find out where Mac is, I'm going down the back if you're happy?" I let the cockpit know. They agreed and I said,

"I am coming off harness and intercom." I've always been told that you keep your harness attached to your body and move the karabiner that secures you to the next D ring attachment on the aircraft. I didn't this time, I took my harness off across my chest as it was the quickest way and I thought it warranted it and looked down the cabin.

It was dark, there were troops and kit around and I fumbled my way towards the aircraft ramp. NVGs were good but close up, looking at objects 6-8 feet or less away, it was very unfocused and blurred. I didn't see the legs sticking out and I tripped up and over onto the floor then, onto the ramp.

I was now on my hands and knees sliding down what I now saw as a dropped ramp. I'd left the horizontal floor of the cabin and was sliding down a 30–40-degree decline. It did pop into my head, well this was a way to go falling off the back of the cab, I wonder how that investigation would go.

My boot got caught and I stopped about two feet from the edge, god, thank you anti-slip flooring. I looked around and saw the curly lead of an interrupter (communications lead from the main aircraft to your helmet) next to the ramp hydraulics.

I plugged in and was linked into the comms with the front end again. I lifted the ramp into the horizontal position with the lever and told the front end that the ramp was now level but no sign of Mac. I looked down by the aft right wheel and I could see Mac's harness, so I thought he must have got off the aircraft to stop the soldier entering under or through the front disc.

I attempted to pull up the harness before we went around again to stop it battering the aircraft skin which would only have damaged and punctured it. It was heavy, and as I peered over the ramp; Mr Mac was spinning two feet under the aft right wheel still attached to the harness. Oh fuck sprang to mind, oh fuckerty fuck.

I informed the cockpit that Mac was hanging underneath the aircraft and had to reiterate that a couple more times for it to really sink in. The Basra massive were getting angry and decided to throw even more tracer at us still in the hover, but they missed. We were just a noise in the sky and luckily, the millilux levels were so low the enemy couldn't determine where we were. Still didn't stop them from having a go.

We had to think of a plan, we couldn't go around as Mac would surely not be at the other end of the harness when we returned to the LS. Lifting him wasn't happening as 17 stone of Jock on one piece of harness next to a 100+ foot drop would endanger everybody else. I decided to brief the crew of two at the front of my plan.

"This is what we are going to do, I'm going to voice marshal the aircraft into the low hover, once Mac touches the ground of the LS I will call height is good. Keep the rear wheels off the ground as Mac may be injured, if he can get loose great if not, I may have to help him. By the way, the last units are going to be very big and very slow."

It was agreed and I counted down from some random number to Mac's feet touching the floor.

"Height is good." Was called by me and Mac started to twist and turn as the harness release had slipped around to his back when he fell out. The aircraft started to drift forward slowly and Mac started to stagger along trying to release his harness.

Mac was still keeping up with the drifting aircraft and I didn't want to put in a 'back one' voice marshal to the handling pilot in case we got into the mixing bowl effect when the pilot doesn't have any references and ends up just going in circles trying to deliver the direction from voice marshalling.

Mac managed to release himself from the harness and fell to the ground clutching his chest. I was still on the ramp and informed the front end, "Mac was clear, clear above and behind." The Captain took the aircraft into the climb and I pulled in the harness and returned to the front right door after lifting the ramp. I reattached myself to the intercom and we went back to the LS.

We landed nose forward again and I went out to greet Mac who, even though hurt, ushered me back into the aircraft. We took the remaining troops and headed back to Basra airfield not before our noisy neighbours presented us with another short burst of tracer.

As we approached Basra, we radioed into our Ops and said we would be shutting down. Ops told us we had been re-tasked, after several radio messages back and forth and without secure comms at that time, we had to go clear and state that we have a Crewman that requires hospital attention. That I am sure woke the Ops room up a little, and we landed and shut down. Once all the passengers were off, Mac went off to the military hospital and I cleared to cab up and put my and Mac's kit and weapons away.

After every sortie, there is a debrief, once I had finished with the kit in the lockers, I was told to report to the Detachment Commanders office (DetCo).

I stepped in and was greeted by the DetCo and our sortie Navigator Flt Lt Chris Middleton was there and no pilot. The DetCo informed me that the Nav had told him of everything that went on and congratulated me on my efforts.

He, however, then warned me that this would stay in-house as the pilot had previously caused some engineering faults and as such the pilots' name had come to the fore at RAF Odiham (home of the Chinooks).

If this was to get home, then the pilot may find his career not progressing much further. He was my boss and as such, I followed what the boss required. On walking out of the room with the Nav, Chris said:

"You know you saved Mac's life."

"I know, at least he can see it out how he wants," I returned.

Mac returned from hospital, I think, the next day, and was extremely lucky, he had severe bruising around his torso but that was it. That harness did exactly what it was supposed to and I am sure there are other crewmen/women out there that have had instances when the harness has stopped them from coming to harm.

New Year was amongst us and even though we had the two can rule (troops were allowed two cans of beer when visiting a purpose built bar) myself and Mac didn't fancy a tin so walked back to the tents. While everybody was celebrating the New Year into 2005, Mac and I started on a couple of 250ml tonic bottles that my sister had sent me.

One containing Bombay Sapphire and the other a single malt whiskey that went to Mac. We had a reminisce about this detachments episode and especially the flight into Basra Palace. Mac mentioned his biggest concern was that we either flew away with him still attached or landed and crushed him under the aft wheels.

For me, this is one of my most defining moments, it was through my intervention that Mac now enjoys retirement. It all boiled down to gripping the situation and staying focused to get it delivered. I put this down to my Aircrew training and the instructors along the way that help build my foundation and taught me the skills to not just deliver but find the best way possible to do so. As the saying goes,

'Every day is a learning day'.

VC10s of 10 Squadron

Life wasn't all Iraq and Afghanistan and other IS infiltrated countries once, but I am sure there are people in the military that have spent well over a decade in the forces that know of nothing else.

There was a time when we travelled the world and completed global exercises. Those days did fade considerably when both Iraq and Afghanistan took hold and I'm not sure they will ever return with the size of the military now. But in the day, we had bases all over the globe where you could be stationed.

What is a VC10? A VC10 was a four-engine jet aircraft that was a revolution of aircraft technology in the 1960s being the fastest commercial aircraft in existence until Concorde took that title and sadly returned it.

Realistically, by the time the RAF finished with them, they were worn out, environmentally unfriendly, inefficient fuel wise and had a very outdated 70s/80s interior which was even worse for the VVIPs.

In its last few years of service, breakdowns were common and stopovers because of this were frequent by airline standards. It was a workhorse that could take passengers, cargo, a mixture of both, complete air to air refuelling and carry an array of dangerous cargo.

It was also utilised as a VVIP aircraft, sometimes for the Royal family, but mostly for the PM, Foreign Secretary and others. While it offered security for those passengers, it also allowed for the ability to travel anywhere at any time.

Try hopping on and off a commercial aircraft to get around the world with a multiple of stops when you want with a rather large entourage in tow.

However, those that flew them thought the aircraft was Queen of the skies and had a soft spot for the old girls. It took the crews around the world and in my four and a half years on board, it allowed me to visit 66 countries.

While some stops were just for a refuel, for others we had long weekends or a week in Washington with a quick shuttle down to Belize and back mid-week. Some countries were fascinating like Mongolia, Yemen and Japan, while others were just stunning such as Canada, Barbados and the Iguazu waterfalls between Argentina and Brazil.

While the work was ordinary and repetitive, seeing those sights and meeting so many people was a great eye opener. From flying the PM one week to having a Sergeant as the highest rank on a planeload of troops the next.

From Northern Norway to South Africa, flying a compete global in just over a week, going from west to east via Honolulu and New Orleans, it was a brilliant time to be flying with exciting destinations and you got paid to do it!

Being privileged to work on the VVIPs allowed for the chance to see so many more interesting countries. In two separate trips with the Foreign and Commonwealth Office, we visited seventeen countries.

Around the Globe on VIP

The first trip saw us travel west to Barbados, Jamaica, Mexico City, Bogotá, São Paulo, Cataratas, Rio De Janeiro, Brasilia, Cochabamba—Bolivia, Roosevelt Roads—Puerto Rico then home.

While the trip was stunning and we had some hours and stays over at certain locations, I think the message from the hotel porter in Rio said it all really, that in some locations you had to have your wits about you.

We were going out of the door to the hotel and walking to a bar/club 300 metres away.

"I'll get you a cab," said the porter.

"No need, it's only a few hundred metres." we chirped.

"See those kids on the corner and the one on the motorbike."

"Yes, but what are a few kids going to do to a large crew like us?" We chimed back.

"Some off you won't make it across the road to get to the club, they'll shoot you first then rob you."

"TAXI!"

However, São Paulo being one of the highest murder rate cities at that time was delightful and we all ventured to a feast and Brazilian dancing cabaret that night. Noisy, delicious and very colourful and that was just the ladies in the cabaret…moving on!

Cataratas had the Iguazu waterfalls or the 'Devils Throat' waterfalls. An impressive mass of water with over 300 different cascades all flowing at once. The FCO was there for talks with the Argentinian neighbours as we were the Brazil side, we just enjoyed the view.

The second was going east this time going to Bahrain, Islamabad, Karachi, Delhi, Colombo, Bangkok, Hong Kong, Tokyo, Ulaan Bator—Mongolia, Novosibirsk—Siberia and home.

I have to say Pakistan was a delight then (1996) and very hospitable people, spoke kindly and affectionately knowing we were British. Tokyo, for the little time we were there was fascinating and a sea of wonder to be believed.

Three of us got caught in the rain whilst walking down a street and a local shopkeeper ran out with three umbrellas and insisted we took them. Once the rain had stopped, we returned them but where else in the world would that happen?

The journey from the airport at Ulaan Bator took us through miles and miles of grassland, rich and vibrant green stretching as far as the eye could see, whole valleys of dense grasslands, stunning, but you felt rather small and out of place being there.

Nearing the Capital, we saw what can only be described as a pollution producer. Some mass concrete infrastructure that belched large quantities of black smoke out of their chimneys and blowing towards the city.

A huge, I assume, fossil-fuelled power station. It looked so out of place is such a peaceful setting and looked very eastern block and very old. The power in the capital was sporadic and while escorting some documents along with an Army Sergeant to the embassy, we were stuck in the lift when the power went off, we eventually made it to the Embassy.

We met two Welsh guys, I think from Bridgend who had been given a building job from their company to come out and complete works around the embassy for a few months. These poor chaps had filled an ISO container with all their work goods and entertainment for a few months, a TV, video player, their own clippers for haircuts, clothes, even a bit of hooch.

The night before they were due to leave, some scumbag had nicked all their items out of the ISO. When they arrived at Ulaan Bator, they found they had nothing. Talk about lads down on their luck, couldn't leave due to visa issues with Russia, had only the clothes they stood up in, had finished the work weeks previously and still had a few weeks left.

They didn't want to get a haircut and possibly get cut as the medical facilities were less than ideal and the food was horrendous. We turn up and start chatting and they were overjoyed to meet someone from the UK.

It used to be that the last night stop-over on a VVIP (not a Royal), the crew and Foreign Office back staff would meet up in one of the rooms the crew were in to have a few drinks and chat about the trip informally.

This was one such occasion and since we had brought a stock of beer and wine from the UK, we filled the bath with ice and let the tins and bottles chill. Having picked up loads of snacks in Japan, we had quite a bit extra.

We invited the two Bridgend lads over who when they walked into the room nearly blubbed when they saw the bath with two cases of Boddington beer. Let's just say the lads enjoyed themselves, we looked after them and made their night.

They swore that they would forever like the RAF and thanked us for making them feel human again. They did try to get on board and kept asking all night for a lift back to the UK, unfortunately, not on this occasion.

While refuelling on the way back to the UK in Novosibirsk, the local authorities stopped anyone from leaving the aircraft. We thought this a bit strange as the ground engineer had to go downstairs to complete the refuel.

There had been an outbreak of the plague in Mongolia and so they didn't want any contamination from us. Mentioning the Foreign Secretary was on board and wanted to stretch his legs had little impact, in fact, he was also banned from even moving down the aircraft steps, just in case he spread the plague.

Tel Aviv—Israel, Amman—Jordan, Jeddah—Saudi Arabia, Damascus—Syria, Aqaba—Jordan, Cairo and Beirut.

Another trip with the Foreign Secretary which was around some unusual places this time. I believe it was in Damascus that the convoy of vehicles with the FCO personnel on board returning to the aircraft sped up to the front of the terminal and the aircraft steps only for the front vehicle to slam on his brakes.

Like a concertina, all the vehicles piled into the one in front which led to the very front one making it through the terminal window, that was a laugh!

Tel Aviv was quite lovely and several of the crew went out to see the lay of the land, beach, café, etc. On hearing some music, we decided to find out where it was coming from. Around a corner was a big stage with lots of people mingling in the street, great we thought, an open-air concert. As we moved to the front we were looking out for the band but couldn't see anyone, must be the warm-up music.

A gentleman nearby leaned into us and gently said in English,

"You should go, this isn't for you." So we were being followed but that happened in so many other countries why different here.

On asking him why, as we wanted to listen to the band (how naive), he informed us that this wasn't a concert but a demonstration against the government and was likely to get violent.

"TAXI."

Real Poverty

Amongst travelling around the Gucci cities of the world, other destinations showed huge chasms in living standards. In Senegal, West Africa, we arrived for a refuel and wanted the steps brought to the aircraft. The airport workers would only bring them in if we gave them all our double bagged rubbish.

By international law, all aircraft refuse has to be disposed of correctly in case of bringing unwanted seeds, or materials that would damage the ecosystem and generally everything is incinerated. Not here, they wanted those bags and we wanted those steps, so there was a swop.

Once the steps were in and they had their huge rubbish bags, those boys were off to the side of the pan splitting the bags and spilling its contents to search for…food. These guys were tucking into what they thought was a feast. Obviously hadn't been paid in a long time or not very much, these people were feeding empty stomachs.

While India may well be fascinating, there is the caste system that denotes what position in society people stand and it also denotes what kind of job those people can get ensuring few rise above their status. I find it hard to compute especially seeing the very poor camped out on the street using a tarpaulin as a home.

It was the professional beggars that astounded me in Delhi, not like the Romanian Gypsies we see in London with a woman holding her baby with her hand out. These families we saw were mostly crippled or deformed and it's done to get people to give more.

We were informed that children have their bones broken at an early age to disfigure them to attract more sorrow and more money. Entire families are brought up to beg as their trade, what a way to live.

To give you how decisions are made in the struggle to live. A family in a poor part of Afghanistan would lose a little girl to disease or accidents and they would mourn. However, if the family lost their only cow then the family would ultimately suffer.

One loss would be hard but could be replaced (the girl), the other would ensure the majority of the family would die through the winter due to starvation. The cow is worth more to the family than the girl. We don't see anything like that here.

Night Fighters

We took the British Army to Gaborone in Botswana for an exercise. As being so far away from the UK, we had a night stop. From the airport and on the journey into town, huge billboards displayed the sorry tale of HIV infection in the country.

Once such billboard told the story of '75% of the sexually active adults in Botswana have HIV', what, how many? We were astounded at the figures and messages being broadcast. This was in the nineties before the medicine had caught up with the disease and offered a life after HIV.

As the airport didn't have any catering facilities, we had to order from the hotel kitchen, 150 food boxes and collect them in the morning. Spending a night in the hotel with its attached casino was slightly unnerving as the number of ladies in the foyer and bar area was higher than expected.

We soon found out that these ladies of the night or night fighters were looking to be your companion for a short while if you get what I mean. We were like a pack of sheep moving as if controlled by a sheepdog. Every time one of the ladies approached, we all moved in the opposite direction.

In the morning, two of us went down to the kitchens for the food, we noticed a few discrepancies and alerted one of the staff. There was a little confusion and lots of apologies and sir-calling but far, far exaggerated.

My response was,

"Mate, stop bowing and don't call me sir, me and you are just the same."

"You not from Johannesburg?" Asked the kitchen guy.

"Nah, we're from Britain," was my reply.

All hell broke loose, some local tongue was used and everybody in the kitchen became very animated and all were smiles.

It was great to see the transformation as if some weight had been taken off their shoulders. We sorted out as best we could the discrepancies and had a great chatty, friendly time. Lots of questions asked of us about Britain which they seemed to love and the kitchen staff said people get treated a lot better in Britain than there.

Our questions to them were about how they were treated and who treats them poorly. No surprise who and being a few miles over the border with South Africa, there were still some that had kept that identity of being greater and more important and that style alive.

However, we did visit Durban on another trip and saw a completely different side to all that around the stadium where everybody was mixing and having a good time.

Travelling around the globe you get the feeling in different places whether you can leave the hotel and look around or shop, party, walk around by yourself or just have to stay close and live in your room.

Having armed guards on the floors and walking around the hotel is a good indicator of, 'it's a shit hole'

Poker Night

We were in the Middle East and had arrived around midnight, not wanting to get to bed straight away we decided to play cards in one of the rooms. We didn't have any matches so we used the next best thing, the aircraft imprest.

Travelling around certain locations, not all agents at the airports take signed documents as payment or even fuel Carna cards. Sometimes, it's the old-fashioned dollar that makes the process happen which means a large amount of cash has to be carried.

We decided to split up some parts and have a few hundred dollars each to play poker. There was, I think, five or six of us that played and we knew the rules. Play with the money but everything gets returned at the end of the night.

A new engineer was travelling with us and he heard about the game. He wanted to join and was letting us know that he played at home and wanted to get involved in our game.

We had a quick chat and said that this crew who are playing, only do so twice a year, we save up and when the trip comes along, we all get the crew together and have a game for a few nights, what a lot of bullshit, it never happened and this was the first time.

We, between ourselves, discussed if we let him in and we win his money, we give it back at the end of the night, we then discussed, what if he wins it, Mmmm. We let him in and played for about an hour and a half. The Captain said that was it for the night and the engineer wanted to keep going, he had lost a bit.

I think the surprise came when we handed back his money at the end of the evening and it was explained much to our amusement.

The next day the Co-Pilot was arranging all the dollars back into correct amounts, can you imagine what the imprest office would say on return.

"Did you use the imprest?"

"Not at all this trip," the co-pilot would reply.

"Then, why are all the notes crumpled?"

Air to Air Refuelling

I think one of the most spectacular things to see, is the Air-to-Air refuelling of fast jets off the wing of a tanker aircraft. Not only are you close up to the fast jet but refilling at the same time.

With the VC10, unlike some other aircraft that offer fuel from a boom from the tail, it refuelled from a hose that would extend out from each wing allowing for two refuels simultaneously. This allowed you to witness the action and take some great pictures.

On some trips over friendly countries, you would also get their fast jets to come and say hello off the wing. It definitely gave you a buzz to watch it.

On one such trip, the VC10 took the families of a fast jet Squadron on board to witness the refuel. Reciprocating the act the fast jet Squadron said that it would take up one of 10 Sqn's personnel.

I remember getting a call while on leave, asking if I wanted a trip, I didn't get the idea, I thought I would be crewing on the VC10, why would I do that on leave. No, no, you'll be in the F3 Tornado they said, time to cancel my leave, I think.

I was looked after and measured and fitted with all the gear including the Anti-G trousers. I was briefed on ejecting if necessary and what not to touch, everything. It was superb, we were on an engineering sortie to test out the new engine that had been fitted.

We departed and went out to the west over the Irish Sea and further north and went through the steps of the engineering task sheet. Eventually, passing the speed of sound and suddenly the entire cockpit going quiet as the sound barrier was broken.

I believe we eventually pushed the jet to about 820 kts, with this vapour halo surrounding the cockpit glass. A few turns at speed and clenching my stomach down and feeling the anti-G trousers inflate to stop the blood moving to your legs and passing out.

We looped the loop, which was absolutely amazing and then went to find the VC10 and took some fuel from the hose. That's some talent to maintain a straight and level at I think 300 kts to get the probe into the basket to get some fuel. I know some instruments can artificially maintain cruise and height but even so, good talent all the same.

It was definitely a day to remember and very grateful for the opportunity once in my life to go supersonic. I only have a hot air balloon and a trip around the moon to go. The hot air balloon will happen someday when it's a special occasion but Elon Musk should help me with reducing the cost of a ticket around the moon because of the free advertising he's received in here.

Things You Do for A Bit of Fun!

We had a gentleman Loadmaster called Mike McKee, he was a big built guy that had completed most of his time on Hercules and as such was quite deaf. He was a very content and happy man that had a very warm and natural friendly nature about him. We used to hit it off and found ourselves travelling many times together over the world.

One of our favourite past times was a beer and a bucket of hot chicken wings while at the local sports bar in America or Canada. We ended up on a very long stay over and hopping around both countries. We also had a little competition about who could eat the hottest wings.

We had been doing this over several months now and found ourselves at a place called Montana's sports bar and for the life of me, I can't remember where the place was (please don't say, Montana!).

We ordered a bucket of fifty chicken wings and a pitcher of beer. The waitress asked whether we wanted the hot, something like the furnace and the volcano! We both, in unison, said the volcano.

The waitress who was only trying to warn us that they were very hot, very, very hot. Did we listen, we pushed aside the warning and explained that we do this every time we come away and haven't had a wing that we couldn't handle. Beers on the table, half a match down and side plates, napkins and finger bowls to the ready. Out came this single bucket of wings and it passed by and onto the table.

Well, I thought I had been stung in the eyes with the chemical reaction as the steam of the wings hit my face. We looked at each other across the table, a nervous giggle from both of us, "you first", "no you first" as we chickened out.

We each took a wing and bit into the meat; it was as if I had been given an anaesthetic and my entire mouth and surrounding cheeks had become numb. I was pushing my skin and pinching my cheeks as I didn't register the touch. I looked up and saw Mike, he was crying, I mean streams of tears were coming down his cheeks.

"You alright Mike, what's up mate?" I slurred.

"My tear ducts have burst; I can't stop crying."

And there we sat like two idiots, one crying his eyes out, the other dribbling because he had no control of his mouth. At the end of the night, we paid the bill but declined the nice offer of a doggy bag for the remaining wings. There sat 48 whole wings and 2 wings with a single bite out of them.

The Balkans

With the Balkan war continuing through the nineties, trips to and from Split in Croatia were commonplace to resupply and as a troop mover. I think on one of these trips it was the first time I had seen a soldier suffering from PTSD as we would call it now. Knowing that he wasn't quite himself, I introduced myself and we chatted, I got him teas with real milk (luxury) and he said he wanted to talk.

The lads around said I should leave him alone as he'd changed, gone off one, not there, etc. Well, I didn't and he told me of a story about a family in a village, he wanted to tell someone and I'm glad he did.

They were in a Warrior APC group who were visiting the Muslim villages in and around Bosnia Herzegovina to assist with a bit of hearts and minds, talk to locals, tell them why they were there, provide some basic medical checks on the families, etc.

As it turned out, they were being watched as a call came in and said they had to exit the town immediately. This soldier was at the time bouncing a little girl off his knee, getting her to laugh with the rest of the family around the house and yard.

They mounted up and as soon as they were out of the town boundary the shells started coming in from the Serbians. After an hour and after the shelling stopped, the troops went back in to look for wounded. The soldier I had been chatting to on the aircraft said he returned to the house where the little girl was. The house was demolished and none had survived.

He was obviously in distress but what did the army have then as a coping mechanism to deal with this, old fashioned get a grip of yourself, great if you are moaning because you are cold and wet, not good in this instance. I always wanted to know what happened to him and if he ever managed to shed that heavy burden.

The VC10s were eventually allowed back into Sarajevo which had not been accessible for some years. Those aircraft from other nations that had tried and mostly failed with skeletons of aircraft on the grass surrounding the runway.

While I had witnessed a lot on TV reference the fighting, mortaring of markets places and snipers constantly shooting civilians in the street who were only trying to shop, I hadn't realised the true damage to the infrastructure.

As we descended I saw thousands of houses untouched and looking quite picturesque and wondered what was going on. Then I noticed on certain hillsides, one group of houses where untouched while on the opposite, every roof and wall were marked by scorching and holes that had destroyed the houses, that was the difference of religion.

Within a few miles of landing in Sarajevo, every single house, hamlet, village, property, barn was scarred or had its roof fall in or walls marked where shells had gone in. It was a total scene of devastation and systematic cleansing of the entire land.

Nothing was left but husks of building now devoid of life. On the airfield French soldiers, I assume Legionnaires were dug in with mortar and weapons at the ready, it was still quite an unreliable peace.

That war eventually finished but not before I covered it with the Chinooks later on.

Central Asia

Finding ourselves delivered to Uzbekistan by the Lufthansa crew as a positioning post for another VIP trip, we found ourselves with a few days off in Tashkent. The Lufthansa crew which stayed once a week were also staying over in another hotel and had a few suggestions on what you could do around the area.

We were all invited to an authentic Uzbekistan meal with a family and a lot of us turned up in the standard run-down minibus. What we didn't know is the story of why we were invited by the Captain and pilot of the Lufthansa crew.

The German Captain during one of his stays over had decided to go skidooing during the winter with another member of the crew. All dressed correctly and each with a skidoo, they left for a trek through the countryside.

On their return as it was soon to get dark, the Captain on the rear Skidoo had an accident and fell off his machine. The front skidoo driver didn't notice until much later but could not remember the exact route they had come and it was now dark and snowing.

The German Captain laid in the snow with some serious injuries that he couldn't manage to get on his skidoo. The temperatures during the winter months and at night would soon claim his life if he didn't get help. He did get help; help came to him in the way of a local man returning to his wooden shack after looking after his animal stock.

The local man was just in the right place and at the right time and rescued the German Pilot and took him into his shack where he cared and looked after the German pilot for three days until he could raise help to rescue the pilot.

Eventually, the German pilot did get rescued and flown to a hospital for emergency treatment. The German pilot has been eternally grateful and as such every time he flies this particular route and stays at Tashkent, he goes to see the man and his family.

Sometimes he goes by himself, others, he takes a group like us. What we did was pay for the privilege of this local man's hospitality and as such help repay a little debt the German Pilot says he owes, we were more than happy.

However, reaching for the large bottle of what I thought was water on the table and pouring it in the large glass that was provided by the family and taking a large gulp, I realised far too late that the large bottle was Vodka and the small bottle was water.

The food was as you would think, designed to stay edible over the winter months so there were a lot of pickles, fatty meats and fresh veg while it lasted. Was this what we would normally eat, no. Was the effort appreciated along with the story, very much so. It's a pity we didn't speak their language or have a device that could translate at the time.

On the same stop over the day before we were due to take over the VC10, we went for a sightseeing tour of Samarkand. This was going to be a long road trip but the chance to see one of the oldest continuously inhabited cities in Central Asia thought to have started around the 7th or 8th century BC.

It also had some very famous mosques that were built by descendants of Genghis Khan around the 9th century that was worth a visit.

We had a very enjoyable day out but were rather weary and all fell asleep on the coach returning us to Tashkent. What happens in many countries when travelling for an unknown reason to me is the drivers turn their headlights off once they have passed a vehicle.

I don't know whether it's for the battery life of night vision but they do. All we knew was we were all awoken by being thrown forward and hearing the scrape and crunch of metal on metal, then it all went silent. Once everybody got their heads together, it was a 'what's just happened' moment.

We had hit a taxi on the road and I'm not sure who hit who or which side of the road anybody was on as there were no lights or ambient light anywhere. We didn't move for ages and we needed to know we could get back to Tashkent for the next day's arrival.

To make matters worse for us, we found out we were in Turkistan. A direct route to Samarkand took us through the country of Turkistan where we were now stuck, without clearance or visas and an irate taxi driver wanting for us to follow him to the local town and get the police involved.

Can you imagine the shit storm when the VC10 landed the next day with the Foreign Secretary and found out the crew weren't waiting for them and even worse not in the same country but prison in Turkistan? There was a lot of talking between all parties, especially our Captain and the bus driver.

Eventually, we paid for the taxi to come with us to a town in Uzbekistan which allowed us the get out of jail card. Once we were over the border then it sorted itself out and we, after a very long day into the early hours, went to bed.

Diana, Princess of Wales

Having travelled through Kuala Lumpur, Jakarta, and at this moment in Manila with the FCO, we thought the turn up to the aircraft to travel to Singapore would be routine as VVIPs go with the Foreign Secretary. This day, however, was going to be as my parents said once, "you knew where you were when it happened" kind of days.

They were referring to the assassination of President Kennedy, but I am sure throughout history, key moments will fall into that category as they still are nowadays. Declaration of war against Germany over the radio in 1939 and the fall of the Twin Towers in New York.

This day was 31 August 1997 and we were at the aircraft already when the FCO staff appeared. The message came down that we were delayed for take-off but no reason why. Some of the FCO staff were in tears and then the press corps turned up at the aircraft since we were flying them alongside the Foreign Secretary.

The captain came down the back of the plane and briefed the crew quietly and informed us that we had a job to do and professional nature to uphold. He then informed us that Diana; The Princess of Wales had been killed in an accident. That was all that we were informed of and told to go about our duties as expected.

It was one of those moments when a collective numbness takes over, people were being comforted on the aircraft, we were completing out checks and looking after the passengers, the press were outside, at the bottom of the steps, waiting for the Foreign Secretary to say something to them.

Because of where the accident happened (Paris), the protocol says that the Foreign Office is the first point of contact. I'm not going into the who got the news first out of anyone, but we heard quite quickly as it was still only early morning in Manila and so the very early hours in Europe.

The Foreign Secretary provided a statement to the press as is required in these matters before he boarded the VC10 and onto Singapore. Once the Foreign Secretary was on board then the press stormed into the plane and this is where I saw the utmost un-glorifying greed and animal, gutter instincts of certain press members.

By far the biggest story of decades, what followed was like a lather of ferocious activity to ensure their story was going to hit the front pages before the aircraft took off. I've never witnessed scenes of such demented behaviour and shouting down mobile phones and such large demands being made to then finish one call to make another.

Unbeknown to us, as we still had a couple more days of travelling to go, was the mood of the country on our return. We missed all the news when we were away and hadn't kept up with anything about Diana's death. When we did return home, it was a bit of a shock to see such an emotional response from the country.

We had been and felt completely detached and what I witnessed on return was astounding. I can't recall an example since, that has matched the overspill in our nation's hearts as much as this. This was my last flight on VC10s before I started my Airman Aircrew training at RAF College Cranwell.

It's All About the Image

On a few occasions, the VC10 had to be pre-positioned at Heathrow on the VIP parking spot near the VVIP terminal (yep, there is a different terminal to the rest).

We, as the oncoming crew had to travel from RAF Brize Norton to Heathrow on the day to pick up the aircraft. I cannot recall the reason for the pre-position or why we didn't fly from Brize to Heathrow now.

We were on our way down the M40 from Oxfordshire when we hit traffic that put us at a standstill. Not unduly concerned initially, as we always were at the aircraft hours before, we just talked amongst ourselves. After twenty minutes, we felt that if this was the speed we were going to go to reach Heathrow then we would be struggling.

After thirty minutes, we started to wonder how we were going to let people know that we were going to be late. This being the 1990s, mobile phones were the size of a briefcase and cost thousands of pounds and only the rich and important had them and to us, that was the London City folk in the banks and exchange.

Low and behold, looking out of the left-hand window of our crew coach, we see a man driving a convertible Mercedes with none other than a big house brick size phone. There he was laughing and chatting into his phone as we sat in the traffic, watching the minutes tick by.

The question was passed to the Captain that why not ask the guy on the phone if he would allow us to use the phone with the understanding that we would pay for the privilege.

I can't remember who went to the driver but I have a feeling it was the Ground Engineer (GE). Off the GE trotted and we could all see he was waved off virtually immediately and he duly returned to the coach.

More discussions amongst the crew of how we were going to explain to the VVIP who happened to turn up at the aircraft, only to find it shut with nobody to fly it.

After another chat, someone else was chosen to go and chat with the guy with the phone but with a bit more emphasis that this would help us and it was possibly helpful to the Government to give it a bit more presence.

It worked, the guy entered a discussion and there was a back-and-forth conversation about the importance of the call. After a few minutes, the plan fell apart and the other crew member entered up the steps at the front door of the coach and we waited for the response, why this turd wouldn't allow us to call our Ops to get the information out.

We were informed that the guy with the phone in the convertible Mercedes didn't want to have anyone use his phone but on the insistence of the second crew members importance of the message being passed, the driver caved in and admitted it was a fake and nothing but a bit of plastic moulded to the shape of a phone.

I wonder how bad he felt when every window on the left-hand side of the coach filled with faces of the crew and he had nowhere to drive off to. We didn't see the plastic phone again and funnily enough, we didn't see him turn his head towards our direction the entire time we were alongside him. That must have been one very uncomfortable drive.

Good end though is, we made it before the VVIP and took off on time.

The Brunei Bailout

Having been woken at 2 am but not required to meet for the crew bus until 10, I found myself dressed and wandering the streets at first light. Walking around Bandar Seri Begawan, Brunei's capital, I ate breakfast out of a banana leaf as I walked through the early morning markets.

Mornings catch of fish were on sale as was any and everything. Meats hanging from hooks, fruit and vegetables I had never seen before and beautifully coloured feathered birds unfortunately in bamboo cages. Fried insects, plastic toys and a lively hub-bub wherever I went.

I came across a river and one of those fast longboats, the ones that are about 20 feet long with a massive engine on the back. I asked the guy if he would take me up the river for a trip. We agreed on a price and I sat up front for the best view.

Off we ventured at a hell of a rate and we passed the jungle, the river and the blue sky, eventually seeing an enormous gold dome appear over the surrounding canopy of the jungle.

It was the Sultan's Palace and very opulent with what I could see. We had travelled about twenty minutes when I thought I had seen enough jungle. I turned around only to see the boat owner bailing out water that was filling up the back of the boat rather fast.

In his hand was an old cut piece of plastic which he was frantically using with one hand while driving and keeping the speed up on the outboard with the other.

He smiled nervously when he saw me look at him. This obviously wasn't the first time it had happened but maybe the last the way the water was coming in. He took his hand of the engine control and used both hands to bail. This had the effect of flattening out the boat as the front end had been lifted out of the water and filling the entire boat with river water.

A certain sense of 'what are the crew going to say when I don't turn up and can't be found'. There was also the realisation that while I could swim, so could a lot of creatures that would like to eat or bite you.

I thought we were going to have to take a swim for the shore which meant jungle. As far as I was concerned, leaving the water would only attract everything else that would want to sting, bite and consume you.

After half an hour, we returned to the starting point near the market, having thanked my guide in saving my life and not allowing anything to get me, I bought a few more banana leaf dishes of fish and rice and chicken and rice and headed back to the hotel.

Tony Blair's Shirt

The newly-elected Labour Party had burst its way on to the political stage in 1997. It seemed a release had happened and the country was inhaling a fresh breath of air. Whatever anybody's politics, this was a dramatic change and it was being led by the new Prime Minister Tony Blair.

During the Conservatives' time in Government, you had information from the cabinet offices on the do's, don't', dislikes and likes. You had lines of communication and faces to name throughout the working process.

Now, everything was new and nothing was known, you had to start from scratch, which worked in our favour as the new government didn't know either.

I was a corporal steward at the time, on the very old and noisy VC10s from 10 Sqn. A throwback to the early 1960s but the fastest commercial aircraft at the time, only beaten by Concorde. It was also used as a large VVIP aircraft for longer journeys or because the entourage was larger than the 32 'The Royal' Sqn BAE 146 could take.

On VIP journeys, it was sectioned off from front to back with the front galley and storage, the VVIP seating and tables, sometimes divan beds followed by the VVIPs office contingent and then the press if we were carrying them and finally the rear galley and a couple of crew seats.

Most of the time the flying was routed and flown so as not to require two divan beds but make room for more seats.

This trip was set to take place around the date of 1 July 1997 or to put it in people's minds of the occasion the Hong Kong handover to the Chinese.

We had been briefed at RAF Brize Norton about the trip and who was going to be on board. I believe it was the PM's first proper long-haul flight with us and as such, all the bells, whistles, etc were being pulled out.

This happened every occasion for a VIP with the aircraft even going into Base Hangar at RAF Brize Norton to be polished on the outside, refitted and carpeted, even the wheels were painted.

We as the crew who would take the PM and the entourage in and out of Hong Kong were positioned in Novosibirsk, Siberia as the crews would run out of legal flying time to take the PM all the way there and back.

Novosibirsk, it was an interesting sight but a lot of what we called Russian building influence, lots of concrete everywhere. We passed blocks of flats, well, when I say we passed, they went on for miles and we found out that a couple of hundred thousand people lived there.

Novosibirsk was home for a few days and we didn't venture far but like always, I'm sure we were followed and kept an eye on as has happened in the past.

It was the 30 June 1997 and we were waiting for the VC10 to arrive so we could change crews and refuel. I was positioned in the front galley with a Master Aircrew (RAF WO1) and we would be the crew for the front eight VVIPs and the cockpit and ground engineers that stayed up the front.

We would also have an Escort Officer from Northolt that was the link between the PMs office and the RAF. The rear crew of a Master or Flight Sergeant and three stewards would look after everybody else.

We had changed crews and I had introduced myself to the PM, Mrs Blair and the Personal Private Secretary and everybody else. It was late at night and we would be getting into Hong Kong early to mid-morning.

The Chinese had stipulated that we would only have 14 hours and 5 minutes on the ground and I mean wheels touchdown, wheels up was going to be 14 hours and 5 minutes later.

A few refreshments were served but then everybody turned in or slept in their seats except the PM and Mrs Blair who each had a divan bed. Probably not the most comfortable place in the world but shut-eye, they achieved.

Before we landed in Honk Kong, I was going to serve breakfast, this included fresh fruit and cooked English, tea, coffee, etc. I had woken the seated sleepers a bit earlier as I had to set up the table with the silver and crockery.

The sleepers awoke and squared themselves away with the washing facilities while we got on with cooking and prepping breakfast. I awoke the PM and left to sort the final parts of breakfast. Mrs Blair joined the table after a while but I couldn't serve until the PM had seated.

Sometime later, the PM came in and I think I had enough time to get at least some food into them before they departed for the handover.

What happened next leaves me in a very awkward position. The Escort Officer invites the PM to the cockpit for the landing into Hong Kong. Those who know Hong Kong now, will know the airport has been built on reclaimed land out to sea.

Before, flying into Hong Kong took you past high-rise blocks of flats that you could literally see into or they could look down at your aircraft. Well, the PM couldn't refuse, might be the last time.

I, however, had to then rush breakfast to the starving seven, fruit salad, cooked, coffee, tea, croissants, jugs of water, juice all put on the table as we had only several minutes before we landed. The door opened from the cockpit, I think it was the Air Engineer and I asked how long we had left, to which he said:

"We're landing now."

We went a bit faster at the front with the Master Aircrew putting everything away and securing the galley and me with a trolley in the VVIP cabin area explaining calmly that we were landing and I had to clear the table and to please fasten their seat belts.

The trolley was half full when the rear tyres of the VC10 hit the runway, I knew what would happen next and just blurted out "grab something". The Captain put on the reverse thrusters and everything on the trolley and the two tables shot forward.

There were several seconds as hands and fingers grabbed, dipped and saved objects from being catapulted from the table. Hurrah, I hear you shout; well, after filling the trolley and using napkins to wipe hands and fingers that entered the condiments (brown sauce) and orange juice, I wheeled the trolley to the galley and we closed the curtain. The Prime Minister exited the cockpit with a huge smile having enjoyed the occasion with the question,

"Have I missed breakfast?"

With the PM's party having disembarked the aircraft, we the crew, set about cleaning and prepping for their return. I stripped the beds and found a shirt the PM had been wearing, thinking it most probably cost a few Bob, so I put it into my bag.

This bag was a present from my twin sister on my 21st birthday and not only did it carry the PM's shirt it carried other items as well, more about that later. Clearing up and polishing the silver etc took a couple of hours due to the lateness of the breakfast service and then we got changed and walked through Hong Kong airport to what we thought would be some transport to a hotel.

We were informed that it was the Hong Kong handover and as such, there were no taxis as it was a holiday. How many times, and I mean, how many times would I hear that today?

We eventually found and caught a bus that dropped us off a quarter of a mile away from the hotel. Checked in and the clock was ticking, we had roughly 11 hours before we took off. With VVIPs you tend to have more work to do, so have to arrive at the aircraft earlier.

So, 11 hours became 8 hours to grab some food and sleep. Firstly, I wanted some dry cleaning done for my shirts and the PM's shirt. I opened my bag and there were my shirts, I pulled out the PM's and for the life of me, I couldn't fathom out the discolouration on his sleeve.

Then, my heart missed a beat as I looked into the bag and saw a huge damp patch on the skin of the bag. The smell gave it away, it was the bottle of Jim Beam that had leaked. As a crew sitting in a foreign country, we had been flown to Novosibirsk by Lufthansa as they were the carrier that could get us there by civilian means.

Transitioning through duty-free, the crew had opted to but a few bottles of an alcoholic nature. You never knew if you were going to get ripped off in these places and considering the standard of food we obtained at some outlets and the cost, we knew we were.

So we carried a few essential ingredients to have a crew room and ensure we didn't walk around parts of the city we shouldn't have. Unfortunately, the cap of the Jim Beam bottle had cracked leaking onto the pigskin leather bag. This had an unfortunate end as the material to touch the wet bag was the PM's shirt.

"Oh fuck, fuck, fuck, fuck, fuck," just kept coming out of my mouth. Here's me some Corporal, fucking up the PM's shirt, there wasn't much of a rank structure divide between us. "Fuckerty fuck, fuck," until an idea entered my head.

I knew, I would call the hotel's laundry service.

"Hello, is that housekeeping, good, can I get some shirts dry cleaned please," I shakily voiced down the line.

"You can," a sigh of relief, "but it will be three days, don't you know it's the Hong Kong handover."

"Yes I do but, it doesn't matter."

"Fuckerty fuck," were some of the expletives venting from my mouth again. There was a knock at the door. I opened it to find a chambermaid asking about my room. God knows what the look of fear and panic on my face looked like, but she knew I wasn't in the best place.

"Where is the nearest laundry to the hotel please," the look of fear starting to encroach on her face.

"Don't you know it's the Hong Kong handover, there be nothing opened." I think the start of a throbbing vein on my temple and the contorted face made her give up some information.

"There's one outside the hotel, out the entrance turn left, first left passed the trainers in the window and the fish swimming opposite and through the alley and at the far end there is one."

It took a few backward, forward moments of questioning to understand where I thought it was. That was me, packing everything into the hotel laundry bag and heading downstairs. I exited the hotel and turned left, literally two doors down is a shop with trainers from floor to ceiling in the shop window (remember this was 1997).

Across the pavement at the start of the alley, was a restaurant with fish swimming in its entire window display, that chambermaid was spot on. I turned down the alley and walked through to a huge courtyard. On each side was a 20, maybe more, storey blocks of flats.

Looking at the far end, I could just make out a hatch that is up like a kebab wagon with its external cover pushed up over the serving area. I went across and saw that it's open,

"Hi, do you do laundry or dry cleaning?" I said looking at rows of shirts and laundry already pressed.

"Yes, what would you like to have cleaned?"

"I have all these shirts but this one has a stain on it."

"We can do that, can you come back in three days?"

"Three days, effing three days! I want it done in three hours."

"Don't you know it's the Hong Kong handover."

"Look, I know it's the Honk Kong handover, that's why I'm here. I'll pay you whatever you need, but I need that before 6 pm tonight."

"OK, be back at 1400."

So, off I went thinking that I had sorted it out and got some food. I passed the street where all I saw was tailors and suit makers. I passed a shop that had famous people in photographs in the window who have previously used the service.

I believe it was Nathan street that I walked through to get some food, a quick bowl of something with noodles and I was back in the hotel. I saw Norman Webster, one of the Loadmasters and mentioned to him what had happened, I think there was a slight paleness to Norm once he understood and he said I had better inform the Escort Officer.

Off I trotted to the laundry down the trainer and fish alley to the kebab house opening at the end of the courtyard passed the huge blocks of flats. I can let you know that there was a mild sense of foreboding and even a bit of leaked gas at this point. I see the vendor and he immediately gets my shirts.

"All good, they've been laundered and ironed," and he handed over the shirts. They did indeed look very well done. He then reached over a pulled a separate white shirt out and said, "but I couldn't get the stain out of this one." Oh my.

Having survived a mild heart attack, I think what the consequences would be for ruining a Prime Minister's shirt. I wasn't concerned about the PM, more the attitude of how the RAF would take it.

I reckon I was in for a real career kicking from them considering the embarrassment that I would cause or their belief. Shit rolls downhill and I was sure some senior RAF Air Officer that shit would get bigger and faster every rank it went passed rolling towards me.

What could I do and walking back through the courtyard I remembered the tailors, well if I can't clean the shirt then can I replace it? I ventured inside the shop which had staff and three customers, one customer left and a couple I think were already being looked after. The shop person asked what I wanted and I replied:

"I want this shirt copied. Can you do that?."

"Yes we can do that but it will be six days."

"Six days, six days, I want in in six fucking hours."

"Can't do that sir, don't you know it's the Hong Kong handover?"

I blurt out, "Yes, I know, that's why I'm here, this shirt is our Prime Minister's, Tony Blair's."

"Isn't he due tomorrow?" said the couple joining in.

"No, let me explain," as I pulled out my RAF ID to reinforce the fact that this was indeed Tony Blair's shirt.

"I am on the crew that brought in Tony Blair, this is his shirt and I am going to be in deep, deep shit if I don't get this sorted. I want the same material, you to

88

take the buttons off and place them on the new shirt, double cuff the sleeves, take the label out of the back of this shirt and put that in the new shirt and make sure the collar is the same size and shape, can you do that?"

"Yes, we will need three machinists working for four hours each but it will cost you 1000 Hong Kong dollars."

I paid on my credit card not even knowing how much that was but it sounded expensive. The tailor took the name of the hotel and said the concierge would let me know when it arrived.

Going back to the hotel, I think I could get at least a couple of hours shut-eye before having to report downstairs. I think I had about 30 minutes in bed before the hotel tower just shook as the £1 million firework display started.

No point staying in bed and I showered and dressed. I got a phone call from the concierge to say that a package had arrived and would be waiting for me downstairs. I decided to go down as I was at a loose end in the room.

The concierge handed me a shirt box, I opened it and was very pleased with myself at the result. Norm had come downstairs and asked how I'd got on. I showed him the shirt and his next question was,

"Where's the old shirt?" Mmmm, hadn't considered that.

The concierge then handed me another box, this I realised was the old shirt and I had a little bit of nervousness catching up with me. I opened it up and compared the two, shit, fuck and shit again. The material they used for the new shirt was shiny not like the cotton, matt, plain shirt from the PM.

With that, the Escort Officer arrived and I was persuaded to hand over both shirts to him. It did cross my mind that I might get away with it but it was insisted upon. Norm and the Escort Officer exchanged talk as I joined the rest of the crew before we headed back to the aircraft. All I could think about was that bloody shirt and how much shit I was in.

We worked on the aircraft and before we knew it the PM and entourage had turned up along with Cherie Blair's brother, Chinese wife and Paddy Ashdown. All seemed in very good spirits and smiles and cheers were all around, the event had gone well, not that we had seen any of it.

Fine claret was passed between the party and there was a buzz about the place. We took off 14 hrs and 5 minutes after landing and reached the top of climb after take-off, I entered the cabin and offered refills. Accepted by some I was just about to leave when the PM said,

"Simon." Shit the bed, I hadn't been called Simon, steward, Corporal or anything on the way out. He knew, he bloody knew and I wanted a big hole to open up in the aircraft and allow me to fall to my death.

I turned and said,

"Yes Prime Minister."

"The Escort Officer has explained to me that there was an accident with my shirt and the laundry had caused my shirt to be damaged." Backpedal, am I going to get out of this, had the Escort Officer covered my arse and most probably the rest of the crews?

"He told me what you had done," he continued "and the fact you haven't had any sleep and went above and beyond what was required of you."

"Yes Sir," I squeaked.

"Well." pulling the old shirt from under the table he said "That's the best service I've ever had, here you go." and with that, he gave me his old shirt with 'To Simon, That's the best service I've ever had. Tony Blair 1 July 1997'.

I left the cabin and Norman Webster; the front loadmaster came up to me and said:

"You fall in a bucket of shit, you come up smelling of roses, well done."

Let's just say, it went down very well and a few on the crew breathed a sigh of relief, none more than me.

The shirt is framed but rarely is seen. This story wasn't told many times by me but some others dined out on it for several occasions and that particular person is now a Yeoman Warder.

It got around certain people that at an RAF conference held by an Air Vice Marshal, two Tornado pilots came up and said:

"Are you the guy with the Tony Blair's shirt."

I've still not had a beer for that.

For information sakes, the 1000 HK dollars worked out at £88. Final point is that the Escort Officer and Captain were so happy at the outcome that I had my money returned by the Flight imprest. The shirt is framed and I received a very complimentary letter from 10 Downing Street.

10 DOWNING STREET
LONDON SWIA 2AA

4 July 1997
THE PRIME MINISTER

Dear Squadron Leader Walsh

Thank you for the most enjoyable flights to and from Hong Kong earlier this week. It was quite an experience sitting in the flight deck for the landing at Kai Tak, and one I will not easily forget.

This was our first experience of a long haul flight on a VCIO with the Royal Air Force, and Cherie and I were most impressed with the excellent service and comfort provided. It was marvellous to have the chance to sleep in a comfortable bed prior to such a long and busy day in Hong Kong.

Please convey our grateful thanks to the rest of the crew, not least to Simon for the new made-to-measure shirt.

Your friendly,
Tony Blair
Squadron Leader J.M. Walsh

Exercise, Exercise, Exercise

Like all other units, Squadrons, Regiments, exercises are the bread and butter of putting all those daily skills into a warfighting scenario. Some exercises were so brilliantly devised, executed and rewarding, the growth, experience level and capacity increased so much, returning to normal duties seemed dull.

Other exercises were nothing but flying empty cabins pretending to have troops or Casevacs on board and just turning up at points as requested.

There were usually two large scale exercises a year in the UK we attended that involved Brigade level movements. These would often start down south, southwest of the country and work their way through Salisbury plain, Carlisle airport and onto West Freugh in Scotland for a major airfield assault.

One time we attacked the airfield at West Freugh with a ten ship (nine Chinooks and one Merlin helicopter) with the Paras on board. The opposing forces on the ground were so dismal that the high-ranking army officer in charge told them they had to do it all again the next day and they had better put up a greater fight in defending the area or they would be having that fight with him.

Tactical Leadership Training TLT

Some exercises were just awesome to get to understand. Every year there are major air exercises held and this particular year I was invited as part of the Chinook detachment. It was the Tactical Leadership Training course for the fast air.

We had two weeks in Scotland with 60 other aircraft and 300 aircrew flying nightly missions to achieve the aim. Every conceivable aircraft were there from Tornadoes, both F3 and GR4, Harrier, AWACS Airborne Early Warning and Command and Control, Hercules, Nimrods, Hawks, Chinooks and in later years, Merlin, Army and Navy Lynx and Sea Kings and Apache.

The first week was a ramp up on training and planning with flying at night. The crews would turn up at 11.30 in the morning and the breakout plan for the Mission Commander would go ahead, that was our signal to go get a coffee and burger. 12.30 everybody was in the initial brief and the mission was explained and the aim was provided, everybody dispersed and started planning.

Every few hours, everybody got together to work out differences, the major one being safety and deconfliction in the airspace. We had a fantastic piece of kit called the TAMPA which was a mission planning aid for the Tornados.

You could input your aircraft type, route, height and speed, the TAMPA would display this on a large map on a big screen. It would have everybody else's type of aircraft and route on there too. The route used to be flown speeded up with us watching as aircraft approached each other at certain times and certain locations.

This TAMPA allowed you to distinguish what the confliction was and as long as the deconfliction could be explained closer up by either distance, height or geographical feature then the plan continued. I have witnessed last minute planning just before the Chinooks got airborne that did not deconflict to the satisfaction of the umpires/staff and the entire mission was canned for that night.

You can't have 60 aircraft flying around trying to dog fight each other over Scotland and ensuring no-one enters Scottish Air Traffic routes and have potentially conflicting points. The final brief sometimes extended for so long, the helicopter crews departed before its end.

We were the slowest asset and it would take an hour or more to get to the destination even before the fast air took off. Being on time at the briefing is important and I have seen crews from specific aircraft late arriving at the main brief and being kicked out of the tent, Wing Commander or no Wing Commander.

By the second week, the crew capacity has increased but so has the level of training. With a four person crew the lead cab most of the time has the Helicopter Mission Commander on the jump seat, the pilot flew, co-pilot on radios all the time and the No1 and 2 Crewman would do the nav from down the back.

Night nav on Night Vision Goggles is standard practice for crewmen and we use 1-250,000 maps for routing and 1-50,000 maps for Initial Point (IP) to target for the last few miles when we go lower level.

At night, we were cleared down to 250ft above the ground but can fly lower with authorisation for specific training. It wasn't the navigation that was the issue, it was getting a break in all the radios to deliver the simplest but most effective navigational direction to the captain.

Add in fast air attacking you, ground-based air defence radar missile systems and troops on board, you tended to get very busy. The last few days culminated in attacking an airfield, usually at Oban, overwater.

We would get hit by everything and anything and would sometimes have to set up a Forward Area Refuel Point (FARP) to refuel the Lynx, Apaches and sometimes us for the practice. Fast air would act as a pre-landing aggressor and bomb to soften up the target. We would have something called a ROZ box (Restricted Operating Zone) in place that would ensure we didn't enter fast airspace before a certain time.

These are used all over theatres to deconflict from ground artillery and other necessities. We would also refuel from a Hercules on the ground doing the same thing. It was an amazing and very educational exercise that drew all types of disciplines and you would return to unit buzzing and with a huge amount of capacity, unfortunately, unless you maintain the rate of experience, skill fade is inevitable.

Saif Sareea 2

Every five years there is a major exercise carried out overseas. Every ten years there is a global exercise that is completed by every section of the British forces (except when fighting major wars with most of your assets anyway).

2001 saw the Saif Sareea 2 exercise start which was to be a desert exercise in Oman for all three services. Us on some of the chinooks were to fly through Europe and meet up with HMS Ocean a Royal Navy Landing Platform Helicopter (LPH) vessel and at the time the biggest vessel the Navy had in RAF Akrotiri, Cyprus. We would also work alongside Sea King helicopters and 40 Cdo Royal Marines throughout the next three months.

Our first night stop was Nice in France but something odd was happening and we couldn't get into the airport and trying to get anything done was really hard work. We had a cab full of gear, engineering equipment, engineers and Squippers for the transit over the Channel and France.

This was 11 September 2001, and then we found a TV in the airport and realised the significance of the Twin Towers coming down. To us, we thought we wouldn't be going on an exercise anymore, we would be heading off to war. The next day, we travelled over to Zante and stopped at Zakinthos for the night.

Realising that once we hit Cyprus, we concluded that we would land on board and depart for some dusty shit hole for a fight. Let's just say, Zakinthos didn't know what hit it. We partied all night, in clubs and bars thinking this would be the last time we would get a chance.

The travelling in the Immersion suit over the water to Cyprus the next day proved to be a very sweaty, stinky and hanging out of your ass type of affair.

We arrived at RAF Akrotiri and eventually got hold of some accommodation, the first thing was to get out of the immersion suit and have a shower as I stank. I had been to RAF Akrotiri several times and knew the layout, what I didn't expect was shared accommodation. So, in I drifted to the shower in my towel and out drifts a female in her towel, Mmmm, smiles all round.

We spent seven days working with the Marines in and around Akrotiri putting in some dust/USL and winching serials all at once.

I also spent a week flirting with this particular female from the shower, as I found out she was there as part of a medical detachment. Who would have thought that we would be married in 2004?

Once on HMS Ocean, we sailed towards Oman and through the Suez Canal, with all that had happened over the previous week in America, marines were positioned on the deck with machine guns and Milan anti-tank missile as a precaution.

The Suez Canal is huge in its length and stature but also has a massive lake in the middle where all the ships pool before heading in the same direction either to the Mediterranean Sea or the Persian Gulf.

The canal is a one-way system, as such, you can only sail one direction at one time a bit like waiting for the car on the opposite side of a humped back bridge to pass before you can go just with lots of ships first.

On HMS Ocean, we were the Tailored Air Group Along with the SeaKings and crews, etc (TAG), you also had the Embarked Forces (EMF) of the Royal Marines and then the Ships Company. There were many clashes between the groups, the main one being that the ship is designed to go from A to B, usually, as quick as it can and that's what the ships' company wanted.

The TAG wanted the ship to change heading and sail into the wind so we could practice Deck Landing Procedures (DLPs) for the helicopter crews day and night and the odd ELVA thrown in. While this was going on, the Royal Marines wanted to use the flight deck as their gym.

It wasn't an easy relationship and nothing like being on board a Carrier Vessel Strike (CVS) or aircraft carrier whose main purpose is the deployment of air assets and looks after you superbly. It defiantly takes a special breed of men and women to join the Royal Navy and go to sea. Three bunks deep and not enough room from mattress to roof of the next bunk to roll over as your shoulders were too wide.

We eventually moved into the desert and joined the very normal temperate climate green 12 x 12s tented city. We made ourselves as comfortable as possible, being an asset that spends its time working alongside the army, we've discovered how to bring everything along with us and survive as a group or individually.

Food was standard temperate ration packs, like lamb stew and chocolate pudding, we were told to bin the pate and cheese as being close to 50 degree Celsius, it may not be safe. The navy had supplied 15 plus chefs for this outfit whose main purpose was to boil water for brews and dipping the ration meals in to heat up. We just threw them on top of the tent and within 15 minutes they were hot enough to eat.

For the first two-three weeks there was no work between 11am—3pm, the temperatures were just too high to operate until you become acclimatised. Laying on your scratcher, you would melt and I'm sure the tents absorbed the heat, it was unbearable for a while.

One afternoon, the engineers came back with the temperature reading from their site, 54 degrees Celsius. With the high temperatures came the cold nights and one such night we found ourselves digging out the only sleeping bags we had, our artic sleeping system.

What we thought was freezing temperatures that had us all hunker down in our artic bags was in fact 29 degrees Celsius. It was the drop in temperature that caused the shivers, not the actual temperature. Water was the issue and we were allocated 2 x 2litre bottles of water a day, you would come back from flying and be pissing marmalade sticks but that was sorted with water bowsers arriving.

From the ration packs, you would have a salt and pepper condiment and a packet of orange flavoured powder to add to the water, we called it screech as that is what your teeth did after drinking it. We used to add the screech and salt and sugar to the water every time, there was your self-made dioralyte and it worked.

I think the thing that was the constant nause was the flies. We had the standard long drops toilets with a plank with holes cut in them and hessian sides and desert roses which were nothing but guttering pipes hammered into the sand for peeing in.

The human body has a wonderful talent at adapting to hostile environments and here the body stopped defecating between 7 in the morning and 7 night or daylight. The reason was that the toilets got so humming that the stench attracted flies and if you had to go you went in the evening when:

a) the stench had subsided because it was cooler and,

b) because the barrier of flies had gone to bed.

If you went during the day, you wrapped a shemagh over your head, mouth and nose, wore sand goggles and walked towards the long drops. Before you were hit by the flies you were retching, then there was the wall of flies that crawled all over you, it wasn't a pleasant experience. You could see the black cloud of flies before you even got near.

The work was tough as the desert is and we didn't have proper techniques for desert landings but they came along. Midway through the exercise, we had to visit an armoured brigade from the army. We stayed for a few hours and found out that half the entire personnel in that army group had come down with D&V.

We didn't want to overstay our welcome so left soon after. At our base called Camp Fairburn, we didn't get sick and we're lucky but it is down a lot of the time to personal hygiene and having the disinfectants and hand gels available to provide that barrier to infection.

Once acclimatised, we were just knuckling down to the experience, body fat disappeared and tans got deeper. Nights were magical as with no light pollution, the skies just gleamed with the millions of stars sparkling. You don't see very much in Europe because of the light pollution but it was fantastic.

Midway through, there was going to be a natural break where everybody went back to HMS Ocean for a few days before resetting for the final few weeks in the desert. We flew the Marines back and then returned for the SeaKing Naval detachment to HMS Ocean.

That was it, we got a message from the ship that they couldn't afford to spend the 4 hours on the Chinook airframes so we had to stay behind in the desert. Comments followed like,

'You're not in a hotel now' etc, etc. We most probably had more effing field time than the entire ship. We wallowed for a bit and then thought bollocks and within two hours we had stripped the camp. Anything that wasn't standard issue, we robbed.

We made flooring for our tents, cupboards, tables and chairs, camouflage netting over the seating area, it was very comfortable but the best bit was the bond between everybody on 18 Sqn. It was a feeling that if you want to rock our boat, we're going to stick two fingers up at you. It was a great time and as a Sqn all of us, whatever trade, became very close mates.

The OC at the time Wg Cdr Dave Prowse had the brilliant idea of buying a long chest freezer when on one of the long trips away from the exercise in Masera. We had ventured there ourselves as it seemed some of the HQ elements for the exercise operated from there. We ate at the camp field kitchen and after two months of temperate ration packs were flabbergasted at the sight of fresh food, I mean lettuce, cucumber, fruit, it made our mouths water.

Back to the freezer, the boss had placed it at the engineers' line and the night before the completion of the exercise and everybody returning to HMS Ocean, he invited the entire 18 Sqn to the line. Nobody had an idea what for and it was a three-line whip, no exceptions, all to go.

On arriving he gathered all of us and complimented all players from the Sqn and invited us to partake in a beer to say thank you. The freezer was full of tinnies and while they weren't frozen, they were cold. It is also surprising how quickly alcohol goes to the head after so long off the hooch.

While many made their way back to the accommodation, myself and the Fluid Druid stayed behind as we would be operating the Chinook next day and so, slept in the back of the cab. While festivities were still ongoing, a game was devised that looked at stealth, agility, strength and guile or to put it another way 'Pallet Sumo'.

We placed a wooden pallet onto a flat surface in the sand. We started with two blokes on the pallet, each would place a booted foot in one of the corners and face off. When the shout went up to start, each bloke would thrust, push, pick up, shove the other with the intention of not being the first one to hit the sand.

Whoever hit the sand first lost, very similar to Sumo with the rules of no hitting the face or neck and no punching. It started well and everybody was getting into the fun. I decided to have a go and was surprised to win, and again, and again.

It went from best of one to the best of three, from two people to four people on the pallet and teams. It all got very serious and even the officers joined in with one dislocating his shoulder and the other dumped on his ass by 2 out of 3 by me.

It was a great experience and after 19 fights or about 30 bouts, I was crowned Pallet Sumo champion by Jimmy Dargue the MC of the evening. I have to admit I was glad it was over as in one of the fights I had landed and hit my Adams Apple and was in some pain.

That night myself and Taff Bence slept on the cab as the start would be early. We were awoken by the pilots turning up and as I put my boots on a jet of liquid shot up my right leg, someone had only pissed in my boot.

So for the next six hours, I flew all and everyone back to HMS Ocean with an essence of stale piss hovering around my general area. Mind you, I think most of the Royals weren't exactly smelling that fresh.

I had been volunteered to stay on the ship for the three-week journey back to the UK, what a mistake that was. We flew 20 minutes in three weeks; the rest of the time was spent in your bunk or the mess. Ships aren't renowned for being quiet and living on deck six under the vehicle storage deck was a pain.

Every two hours, the junior rates on duty would undo the chains that secured the vehicles, drop them on the metal floor or drag them and then reattach them. This floor was your roof and so, every two hours the same thing happened and you woke up.

Initially, it scared the shit out of you as an almighty crash of metal on metal woke you from slumber, bolt upright, banging your head of the roof or the bunk above you. Eventually, like everything, the body adapts and you learn to dismiss the noise; there is certainly a difference to the quietness in the middle of the desert and HMS Ocean.

Once close enough, we couldn't wait to fly off the deck and get back home leaving all the rest at sea with a day to go. HMS Ocean not being the fastest vessel I've travelled on, could in theory travel at 18-19 knots but rarely did.

If it continued at that speed the inevitable "mechanical breakdown, mechanical breakdown, mechanical breakdown" would echo through the ship's tannoy system and then the essence of where the problem was would follow "mechanical breakdown in No1 engine" – it was common and frequent.

The vessel also had a high step on deck five (deck five ran around the entire ship), where the bow of the ship met the main length of the fuselage as both parts were engineered separately but didn't fit, what a joke.

HMS Ocean in America

It wasn't going to be the only time I spent on HMS Ocean and another exercise in the summer of 2004 saw us deploy with a major exercise in the USA. What started as a major exercise before we sailed, thinned out for us by the time we took the three weeks to cross the Atlantic. We arrived at the northeast side of the states and carried out an amphibious and air assault onto a beach and inland.

There was a lot of trooping and underslung loads, one of which caused a bit of a chat with the French. We were due to deploy a French reconnaissance force with their small armoured scout vehicles, these could only fit three soldiers in at a squeeze.

These were like mini tanks but without the turrets and you could fit one in the Chinook. We boarded the troops at the front, drove one of the vehicles into the rear of the cabin and restrained it. Being so close to the roof and back of the cab, the driver had to stay in the vehicle.

Andy Whelam Jones (Whelly Boot) the other crewman was No1 crewman and would look after the other underslung reconnaissance vehicle on a 3m strop to the centre hook. We were all ready and lifted off the deck and positioned ourselves over the vehicle.

The hookers attached the vehicle rigging to our 3m strop and we gently climbed taking the strain on the rigging. As the rigging became taught, a pair of hands gripped the vehicle wheel.

The bloody French had hidden a soldier in the vehicle because of the difficulty in getting in and out once all the kit was in there. They thought it a good idea to have the driver in place as we carried the vehicle underneath the helicopter. Whelly Boot shouted up,

"I can see a pair of hands."

"What you talking about Whelly?"

"A pair of hands on the steering wheel."

"We know, he can't get out."

"No, the one underslung."

That caused a slight panic and we put the vehicle down on the deck and landed again and waited for the soldier to get out before we picked it up and took it inland.

What was that soldier thinking, if we had to get rid of the load because it was unstable, then he was going to Davy Jones locker at the bottom of the Atlantic. I bet it seemed a good crack at the time with his fellow soldiers.

Docking in Norfolk Virginia at the United States Naval base was something else. HMS Ocean was parked in one of the bays and fitted under the flight deck overhang of one of the American aircraft carriers.

The carrier was huge and looked in comparison that it was an older brother looking after its very small younger sibling, we were tiny in comparison and HMS Ocean was the largest vessel in the Royal Navy at the time.

The docking coincided with an outbreak of mumps and all those on board had to stay in quarantine while those on shore had to stay away, down the pub we went.

Having a long weekend, four of us hired a car and visited Washington DC. We found it hard to get accommodation but were soon to realise it was National Weekend when thousands of motorbikes and visitors hit DC. It also coincided with the 17-year wake up of the Cicadas which were everywhere.

These creatures had bulbous red eyes and were bigger than anything the UK has as an insect, not the most attractive of creatures to keep landing on you. Great weekend, all over too quickly before we headed back to the noisy tin can/roll-on/roll-off car ferry!

Arctic Training

Norway is used by the helicopter force as a snow training destination. Before you can even take off, there has to be the mandatory snow survival drills. This used to take three days but has been I believe extended to five or seven. The luxury being, you don't have to do the ice plunge into the water with your kit on and trying to extract yourself from a hole in the ice while catching your breath due to cold water shock.

We were taught by the 'Pathfinders', a group of specially trained Paras with their RSM as chief instructor. Excellent few days with loads of 'Gucci' tips on survival, lighting fires in the cold and wet, gaining insulation and cover from the elements by using the exact stuff you were worried about, snow and ice.

Camping and night navigation and then the impressive, dig yourself a snow hole for four people and include a vent in the roof and a carbon dioxide lane and a candle shelf.

The vent kept the oxygen coming into the snow hole, the carbon dioxide lane was always lower than the sleeping shelf as CO_2 is heavier than air and a candle was lit and watched in shifts as, if it started flickering, then the CO_2 level was too high and we would evacuate.

Everything you did in artic conditions took longer and you had to add extra time on for everything, briefing, planning, getting kitted up, pre-flight walk around, remember the doors of the helicopter stayed open, if you had troops you picked up from the snow.

If they were covered in snow and ice themselves, there is no point defrosting them to make them cold and wet and then drop them off again. They even taught us how to langlauf or cross-country ski, well I say taught, some of us were like the slippy slide brothers covering ten times the distance as everyone else was.

What it taught me was to always have a nutty bag on your person, in your smock. I had kilos of chocolate and toffee with nuts and still lost weight out there.

Flying Training

As with any piece of kit the forces own, unless you practice with that asset and use it in different, difficult and demanding situations, you'll never get the feel of what it can do and how you can manipulate it to its best. The helicopter is no different, it just takes more time to practice and costs a lot more to use.

Getting the crew to work in synergy has its major advantages. The crewman is the eyes and ears for the front end and for example, while you are voice marshalling the pilot to place a rear tyre of the Chinook on a rock at night to drop off troops on top of a mountain, they are looking into the abyss 3,000 feet below to the valley floor without any visual references and the cliff face at the back of the ramp. It doesn't work unless you all work together.

Clinical Research

From shell shock and war neurosis
to posttraumatic stress disorder: a history
of psychotraumatology
Marc-Antoine Crocq, MD; Louis Croc

The term posttraumatic stress disorder (PTSD) has become a household name since its first appearance in 1980 in the third edition of the Diagnostic and Statistical Manual of Mental Disorders (DSM-III) published by the American Psychiatric Association. In the collective mind, this diagnosis is associated with the legacy of the Vietnam War disaster. Earlier conflicts had given birth to terms, such as "soldier's heart," "shell shock," and "war neurosis." The latter diagnosis was equivalent to the névrose de guerre and Kriegsneurose of French and German scientific literature.

This article describes how the immediate and chronic consequences of psychological trauma made their way into medical literature, and how concepts of diagnosis and treatment evolved over time.

Keywords: posttraumatic stress disorder; shell shock; psychotraumatology; literature; history of medicine

Author affiliations: FORENAP – Institute for Research in Neuroscience and Neuropsychiatry, Rouffach, France (Marc-Antoine Crocq); and Cellule d'Urgence Médico-Psychologique, SAMU de Paris, Hôpital Necker, Paris France (Louis Crocq)

Address for correspondence: Centre hospitalier, FORENAP, BP 29, 68250 Rouffach, France
(e-mail: macrocq@forenap.asso.fr)

Epics and Classics

Mankind's earliest literature tells us that a significant proportion of military casualties are psychological, and that witnessing death can leave chronic psychological symptoms. As we are reminded in Deuteronomy 20:1-9, military leaders have long been aware that many soldiers must be removed from the frontline because of nervous breakdown, which is often contagious:

When thou goest out to battle against thine enemies, and seest horses, and chariots, and a people more than thou … the officers shall say, What man is there that is fearful and fainthearted? Let him go and return unto his house, lest his brethren's heart faint as well as his heart. (King James Version)

Mankind's first major epic, the tale of Gilgamesh, gives us explicit descriptions of both love and posttraumatic symptoms, suggesting that the latter are also part of human fundamental experience. After Gilgamesh loses his friend Enkidu, he experiences symptoms of grief, as one may expect. But after this phase, he races from place to place in panic, realizing that he too must die. This confrontation with death changed his personality.

The first case of chronic mental symptoms caused by sudden fright in the battlefield is reported in the account of the battle of Marathon by Herodotus, written in 440 BC (History, Book VI, transl. George Rawlinson):

A strange prodigy likewise happened at this fight. Epizelus, the son of Cuphagoras, an Athenian, was in the thick of the fray, and behaving himself as a brave man should, when suddenly he was stricken with blindness, without blow of sword or dart; and this blindness continued thenceforth during the whole of his afterlife. The following is the account which he himself, as I have heard, gave of the matter: he said that a gigantic warrior, with a huge beard, which shaded all his shield, stood over against him; but the ghostly semblance passed him by, and slew the man at his side. Such, as I understand, was the tale which Epizelus told.

It is noteworthy that the symptoms are not caused by a physical wound, but by fright and the vision of a killed comrade, and that they persist over the years. The loss of sight has the primary benefit of blotting out the vision of danger, and the secondary benefit of procuring support and care. Frightening battle dreams are mentioned by Hippocrates (460?–377 BC), and in Lucretius' poem, De Rerum Natura, written in 50 BC (Book IV, transl. William Ellery Leonard):

The minds of mortals … often in sleep will do and dare the same … Kings take the towns by storm, succumb to capture, battle on the field, raise a wild cry as if their throats were cut even then and there. And many wrestle on and groan with pains, and fill all regions round with mighty cries and wild, as if then gnawed by fangs of panther or of lion fierce.

This text shows very vividly the emotional and behavioural reexperiencing of a battle in sleep. Besides Greco-Latin classics, old Icelandic literature gives us an example of recurring nightmares after battle: the Gísli Súrsson Saga tells us that the hero dreams so frequently of battle scenes that he dreads obscurity and cannot stay alone at night.

Jean Froissart (1337?–1400/01) was the most representative chronicler of the Hundred Years' War between England and France. He sojourned in 1388 at the court of Gaston Phoebus, Comte de Foix, and narrated the case of the Comte's brother, Pierre de Béarn, who could not sleep near his wife and children, because of his habit of getting up at night and seizing a sword to fight oneiric enemies. The fact that soldiers are awakened by frightening dreams in which they reexperience past battles is a common theme in classical literature, as, for instance, Mercutio's account of Queen Mab in Shakespeare's Romeo and Juliet (I, iv):

Sometime she driveth o'er a soldier's neck,
And then dreams he of cutting foreign throats,
Of breaches, ambuscadoes, Spanish blades,

Of healths five fathom deep; and then anon,

Drums in his ear, at which he starts and wakes, And being thus frighted, swears a prayer or two,

And sleeps again,

Etiologic hypotheses were put forward by army physicians during the French Revolutionary wars (1792-1800) and the Napoleonic wars (1800-1815).They had observed that soldiers collapsed into protracted stupor after shells brushed past them, although they emerged physically unscathed. This led to the description of the "vent du boulet" syndrome, where subjects were frightened by the wind of passage of a cannonball. The eerie sound of incoming shells was vividly described by Goethe, in his memoirs of the cannonade at the battle of Valmy in 17921 "The sound is quite strange, as if it were made up of the spinning of a top, the boiling of water, and the whistling of a bird." In the same text, Goethe gives an account of the feelings of derealization and depersonalization induced by this frightening environment:

I could soon realize that something unusual was happening in me ... as if you were in a very hot place, and at the same time impregnated with that heat until you blended completely with the element surrounding you.

Your eyes can still see with the same acuity and sharpness, but it is as if the world had put on a reddish-brown hue that makes the objects and the situation still more scary ... I had the impression that everything was being consumed by this fire ... this situation is one of the most unpleasant that you can experience.

The Dawn of Modern Psychiatry

The psychiatrist Pinel is often depicted as freeing the insane from their chains; in his treatise entitled Nosographie Philosophique (1798), he described the case of the philosopher Pascal who almost drowned in the Seine when the horses drawing his carriage bolted. During the remaining eight years of his life, Pascal had recurring dreams of a precipice on his left side and would place a chair there to prevent falling off his bed. His personality changed, and he became more apprehensive, scrupulous, withdrawn, and depressive. From his experience with patients shocked by the events and wars of the French Revolution, Pinel wrote the first precise descriptions of war neuroses—which he called "cardiorespiratory neurosis"— and acute stuporous posttraumatic states— which he called "idiotism."

The Industrial Revolution and the introduction of steam-driven machinery were to give rise to the first civilian man-made disasters and cases of PTSD outside the battlefield. The public's imagination was struck by the first spectacular railway disasters, and physicians at the time were puzzled by the psychological symptoms displayed by survivors. Very soon, a controversy pitted the proponents of the organic theory, according to which the mental symptoms were caused by microscopic lesions of the spine or brain (hence the names "railway spine" and "railway brain"), against those who held that emotional shock was the essential cause and that the symptoms were hysterical in nature. This controversy was to last until World War I. It seems that the first mention of the term "traumatic neurosis" dates from that time: it was the title given in 1884 by the German physician Hermann Oppenheim[2] to his book containing a description of 42 cases caused by railway or workplace accidents. This new diagnosis was vehemently criticized by Charcot who maintained that these cases were only forms of hysteria, neurasthenia, or hystero-neurasthenia[3]. After Charcot's death in 1893, the term traumatic neurosis made its way into French-language psychiatry: witness the Belgian psychiatrist Jean Crocq4 who in 1896 reported 28 cases caused by railway accidents. It is at the time of Charcot's famous Tuesday's lectures that Janet (1889) and Freud (1893) discovered traumatic hysteria with all its correlates: the dissociation caused by trauma, the pathogenic role of forgotten memories, and "cathartic" treatment. This was a first glimpse of what would later be known as the unconscious.

The Russian-Japanese war (1904-5) was marked by the siege of Port Arthur and the naval battle of Tsushima. It was probably during this conflict that post-battle psychiatric symptoms were recognized for the first time as such by both doctors and military command. Russian psychiatrists—notably Avtocratov, who was in charge of a 50-bed psychiatric clearing hospital at Harbin.

Manchuria—are credited with being the first to develop forward psychiatric treatment. This approach may have been a response to the difficulty of evacuating casualties over huge distances at a time when the Trans-Siberian Railway was not yet completed. Whatever the initial reason, forward treatment worked, and would again be confirmed as the best method during succeeding conflicts. The number of Russian psychiatric casualties was much larger than expected (1500 in 1904 and 2000 in 1905) and the Red Cross Society of Russia was asked to assist.

The German physician Honigman served in this body, and he was the first to coin the term "war neurosis"

[Kriegsneurose] in 1907 for what was previously called "combat hysteria" and "combat neurasthenia"; also, he stressed the similarity between these cases and those reported by Oppenheim after railway accidents[5].

World War I

Psychiatric casualties were reported very early in the war, in numbers that no-one had anticipated. The French physician Milian reported four cases of "battle hypnosis" following military actions in 1914[6]. The well-known German psychiatrist Robert Gaupp reported in 1917:

The big artillery battles of December 1914 ... filled our hospitals with a large number of unscathed soldiers and officers presenting with mental disturbances. From then on, that number grew at a constantly increasing rate. At first, these soldiers were hospitalized with the others ... but soon we had to open special psychiatric hospitals for them. Now, psychiatric patients make up by far the largest category in our armed forces ... The main causes are the fright and anxiety brought about by the explosion of enemy shells and mines, and seeing maimed or dead comrades ... The resulting symptoms are states of sudden muteness, deafness ... general tremor, inability to stand or walk, episodes of loss of consciousness, and convulsions.

In his review of 88 cases of mental disorder in 1915, the French psychiatrist Régis had expressed a very similar opinion about the etiological role of witnessing the horrible death of comrades: "20% only presented with a physical wound, but in all cases fright, emotional shock, and seeing maimed comrades had been a major factor."

The clinical picture of war neuroses differed only slightly in the two World Wars.

In the British military, patients presenting with various mental disorders resulting from combat stress were originally diagnosed as cases of shell shock, before this diagnosis was discouraged in an attempt to limit the number of cases. It is not known when the term began to be used.

According to Merskey,8 the first mention may be a story published in the Times on February 6, 1915, indicating that the War Office was arranging to send soldiers suffering from "shock" to be treated in special wards at the National

110

Hospital for the Paralyzed and Epileptic, in Queen Square. Also in February 1915, the term shell shock was used by Charles Myers in an article in The Lancet to describe three soldiers suffering from "loss of memory, vision, smell, and taste."9,10 Myers reported on three patients, admitted to a hospital in Le Touquet during the early phase of the war, between November 1914 and January 1915. These patients had been shocked by shells exploding in their immediate vicinity and presented with remarkably similar symptoms. According to Myers, these cases bore a close relation to "hysteria."

The first two patients were transferred to England for further treatment after a couple of weeks (the third was still being treated in Le Touquet when the article was published). As we shall see below, these patients might not have been evacuated to the peaceful surroundings of their home country had they sustained their wounds a year later.

Forward Treatment

Indeed, the experience of the first war months and the unexpected large influx of psychiatric casualties led to a change in treatment approaches. The evacuation of psychiatric casualties to the rear became less systematic as the experience of the remaining war years convinced psychiatrists that treatment should be carried out near the frontline, and that evacuation only led to chronic disability. It was noticed that soldiers treated in a frontline hospital, benefiting from the emotional support of their comrades, had a high likelihood of returning to their unit, whereas those who were evacuated often showed a poor prognosis, with chronic symptoms that ultimately led to discharge from the military. Also, it was discovered that prognosis was better if the convalescing soldiers remained in the setting of the military hierarchy,

rather than in a more relaxed hospital environment Thus, by the end of 1916, evacuations became rare and patients were treated instead in forward centres, staffed by non-commissioned officers (NCOs), within hearing distance of the frontline guns and with the expectation of prompt recovery.11 Treatment in the forward area (psychiatrie de l'avant) became the standard treatment, along with the five key principles summarized in 1917 by the American physician Thomas W. Salmon,12 chief consultant in psychiatry with the American Expeditionary Forces in France: immediacy, proximity, expectancy, simplicity, and centrality. Immediacy meant treating as early as possible, before acute stress was succeeded by a latent period that often heralded the development of chronic symptoms; proximity meant treating the patient near the frontline, within hearing distance of the battle din, instead of evacuating him to the peaceful atmosphere of the rear, which he would, understandably, never wish to leave; expectancy referred to the positive expectation of a prompt cure, which was instilled into the patient by means of a persuasive psychotherapy; simplicity was the use of simple treatment means such as rest, sleep, and a practical psychotherapy that avoided exploring civilian and childhood traumas; finally, centrality was a coherent organization to regulate the flow of psychiatric casualties from the forward area to the rear, and a coherent therapeutic doctrine adopted by all medical personnel. Salmon's principles were discovered independently and applied universally by all warring sides; only to be forgotten, and rediscovered again, during World War II.

Among the many treatment applied to stress disorders, one was much used during WWI, and scarcely at all during WWII: the application of electrical current, also called faradization. This was probably because motor symptoms, such as tremor, paralysis, contractions, limping, or fixed postures, were common during WWI, and rare in WWII. Faradization was criticized in post-war Austria; Wagner-Jauregg—a professor of psychiatry in Vienna who was awarded a Nobel prize in 1928—was even accused of excessive cruelty in the administration of this treatment and had to appear before an investigation committee, in which Sigmund Freud had the more enviable role of testifying as an expert.13 A most radical description of electrotherapy was published in 1916 by Fritz Kaufmann,14 in which he explained how war neuroses could be treated in one session only by combining suggestion, authority, and steadfast application of electricity until the symptoms subsided—a form of fight at outrance.

Concussion, Fright, Or Malingering

Aetiology was a controversial question that was reflected by the choice of terms: shell shock or war neurosis? Soma or psyche? The now obsolete term shell shock, harking back to the vent du boulet of the Napoleonic wars, implied a somatic aetiology, such as microscopic brain lesions due to a vascular, meningeal, white or gray matter concussion. Other diagnoses were also used to express the belief that the cause was more an emotional stressor, rather than a physical concussion. Such diagnoses were, for instance, war neurasthenia and war psychoneurosis, in France.

Emil Kraepelin (1856–1926), without doubt one of the most influential psychiatrists of our times, wrote about his experience with war neuroses during WWI in his autobiography, published posthumously in German in 1983: [As early as 1917], the question of war neuroses was raised. We alienists all agreed that we should try to limit an excessively liberal granting of compensations which might lead to a sharp rise in the number of cases and claims … the fact that all kinds of more or less severe psychiatric symptoms could lead to a lengthy stay in a hospital, or even to a discharge from the military with a generous disability pension, had disastrous consequences. This was compounded by the population's feeling of pity for the seemingly severely ill "war-shakers" [Kriegszitterer], who drew attention to themselves on street corners and used to be generously rewarded. In such circumstances, the number of those who believed that a "nervous shock," or, especially, having been buried alive, entitled them to discharge and continuous support, increased dramatically.

Kraepelin's comments typify the controversies that raged at the time: (i) were the mental symptoms nothing more than malingering, with the clear objective of getting away from the frontline? Some 346 British and Commonwealth soldiers were actually shot on the orders of military command and this number certainly included soldiers suffering from acute stress disorder who walked around dazed or confused and were accused of desertion or cowardice; (ii) Did posttraumatic symptoms have pathoanatomical explanations? For instance, were they produced by a concussion of the brain or strained nerve fibres, as had been hypothesized in previous decades for the "railway spine" resulting from train accidents? (iii) A third explanation was a psychological origin—in that case, was the psychological cause limited to the overwhelming fright constituting the trauma, or was it necessary to delve further into the patient's previous personality? The cases of war neurosis observed during WWI were indeed a challenge to psychoanalytical theories; it was simply unbelievable that all cases were caused by childhood traumas and it had to be admitted that psychological symptoms could be produced by recent traumas. Freud had postulated that dreams were a wish fulfilment. Not until 1920, in an address at an international congress of psychoanalysts, did he allow one exception: the case of traumatic dreams, dreams that recall recent accidents or childhood traumas. And even this turned out to be no real exception at all: Freud eventually understood traumatic dreams as fitting into his wish-fulfilment theory of dreams in that they embodied the wish to master the trauma by working it through.

World War II

A dreadful invention of WWII was the concept "total war," with the systematic targeting of civilian populations, as exemplified by the millions of deaths caused by the Holocaust, the air raids on cities to break the morale of civilian populations, and the atomic bombs dropped over Hiroshima and Nagasaki. Despite WWI, most armies were once again unprepared for the great number of psychiatric casualties and psychiatrists were often viewed as a useless burden, as exemplified by a memorandum addressed by Winston Churchill to the Lord President of the Council in December, 1942, in the following terms:

I am sure it would be sensible to restrict as much as possible the work of these gentlemen [psychologists and psychiatrists] … it is very wrong to disturb large numbers of healthy, normal men and women by asking the kind of odd questions in which the psychiatrists specialize.

American Psychiatry

American psychiatrists made a major contribution to the study of combat psychiatry during WWII. In Psychiatry in a Troubled World, William C. Menninger shows how the lessons of WWI seemed at first to have been entirely forgotten by the American military: "during the initial battles in Africa, psychiatric casualties were sent back to base hospitals, often hundreds of miles from the front. Only 5% of these were able to return to duty." As explained by Jones,19 American planners, under the guidance of Harry Stack Sullivan, had believed that potential psychiatric casualties could be screened out prior to being drafted. Correspondingly, no psychiatrists were assigned to combat divisions and no provision for special psychiatric treatment units at the field army level or communications zone had been made. The principles of forward treatment were rediscovered during the North Africa campaign in 1943. Advised by the psychiatrist Frederick Hanson, Omar N. Bradley issued a directive on 26 April 1943, which established a holding period of 7 days for psychiatric patients at the 9th Evacuation Hospital, and for the first time the term "exhaustion" was prescribed as initial diagnosis for all combat psychiatric cases.20 This word was chosen because it was thought to convey the least implication of neuropsychiatric disturbance. Beginning in 1943, treatment in the forward area similar to that in WWI was the rule, with the result that between 50% to 70% of psychiatric casualties were able to return to duty. Here again, the sheer number of psychiatric casualties was staggering. For the total overseas forces in 1944, admissions for wounded numbered approximately 86 per 1000 men per year, and the neuropsychiatric rate was 43 per 1000 per year.

In 1941, the first year of the war for the United States, Abram Kardiner—famous for having been analysed by Freud himself—published a book based on his treatment of WWI veterans at Veterans Hospital No. 81 between 1922 and 1925.21 In the light of the experience with WWII soldiers, Kardiner published a revised edition of his book at the end of the war.22 He wrote that "the real lesson of WWI and the chronic cases was that this syndrome must be treated immediately to prevent consolidation of the neurosis into its chronic and often intractable forms." He identified traumatic neurosis as a "physioneurosis," thereby stressing the concomitance of somatic and psychological symptoms. Kardiner developed his own concept of the "effective ego" and he postulated that "ego contraction" was a major mechanism.

Posttraumatic psychiatric symptoms in military personnel fighting in WWII were reported as early as 1945 by the American psychiatrists Grinker and Spiegel.23 Their book—Men under Stress—is an excellent reflection of psychiatric thinking of the time; it remained a classic treatise on war psychiatry because of its detailed description of 65 clinical cases, its reference to psychoanalytical theories, and the description of cathartic treatment by "narcosynthesis" using barbiturates. Grinker and Spiegel distinguished acute "reactions to combat" from delayed "reactions after combat." The latter included "war neuroses," designated by the euphemism "operational fatigue" syndrome in the Air Force. Other chronic consequences of combat included passive-dependent states, psychosomatic states, guilt and depression, aggressive and hostile reactions, and psychotic-like states.

European Studies

Long-lasting psychological disorders were not tolerated in the German military during WWII, and official doctrine held that it was more important to eliminate weak or degenerate elements rather than allow them to poison the national community. Interviews we conducted with Alsatian veterans who had been forcibly drafted into the Wehrmacht taught us that soldiers who had suffered acute combat stress (such as being buried under a bunker hit by a bomb) were given some form of psychological assistance soon after rescue; they were typically sent to a forward area first aid station (Verbandsplatz) where they received milk and chocolate and were allowed to rest. The Soviet army evolved its own system of forward treatment, under the responsibility of the unit's political (i.e., morale) officer.24 A look at the textbook of psychiatry published by Gurevich and Sereyskiy25 in Moscow immediately after the war in 1946, at the height of Stalin's power, shows the existence of a specific diagnostic label to classify posttraumatic disorders. The authors describe the "affective shock reactions" (affektivno-shokovye reaktsii), a subtype of psychogenic reactions, that are observed after wartime events, earthquakes, or railway accidents; these are characterized by acute (a few days) and subchronic (a few months) symptoms. These Russian authors tended to emphasize cardiovascular and vasomotor symptoms, which reminds us of Da Costa's "irritable heart" in American Civil War soldiers. The literature on Holocaust and concentration camp survivors is too abundant to be summarized here. The best known of all the early works studying concentration camp survivors is probably the article published by Eitinger.

In contrast to WWI, the course of symptoms over decades and their chronic nature were extensively studied in WWII survivors. For instance, in 1988, we studied a group of French civilians living in the Alsace-Lorraine region who were conscripted into the German army and later held in captivity in Russia. This population of Alsace-Lorraine was interesting because it was bilingual, French and German, and had cultural roots in both heritages. The analysis of 525 questionnaires showed that, after over four decades, 82% still experienced intrusive recollections and nightmares of their wartime captivity; 73% actively attempted to avoid thoughts or feelings associated with the trauma; 71% reported a foreshortened sense of the future; and nearly 40% reported survivor guilt. Beyond PTSD, these survivors from Alsace-Lorraine also suffered lasting personality changes. We believe that an aggravating factor was the fact that these individuals returned home uncelebrated, embittered, psychologically isolated, and that they were caught in a web of psychological ambiguity. They had fought in the German army against their will and under the threat of their families being

116

deported, and were considered unreliable by the Germans. They were surprised to be treated as German soldiers upon their capture by the Soviet army.

They were repatriated to a new post-war social environment in a French society that was itself plagued by the guilt of its early surrender to the Nazis, and they felt misunderstood by some of their countrymen who criticized their incorporation into the German military as a form of treason.

The Vietnam War

During the Vietnam war, the principles of treating psychiatric casualties in the forward area were successfully applied, with a correspondingly low level of acute psychiatric casualties (11.5 per 1000 men per year). In contrast, the incidence of alcoholism and drug abuse was high. Similarly, the late and delayed effects of combat exposure in the form of PTSD were a significant source of suffering and disability among veterans in the United States. An estimated 700 000 Vietnam veterans—almost a quarter of all soldiers sent to Vietnam from 1964 to 1973—required some form of psychological help. The prevalence of delayed and chronic PTSD, in spite of the careful prevention of psychiatric casualties in Vietnam itself, was a rude awakening. Trying to explain this paradox called for new hypotheses, for instance, that PTSD might be a common form of psychiatric casualty in "lowlevel" warfare.28 Similar profiles had been observed in the French post-colonial wars in Indochina and Algeria. This post-Vietnam syndrome, increasingly diagnosed in veterans in the seventies, ultimately led to the adoption of PTSD as a diagnostic category in 1980 in DSM-III. It seems puzzling that no such category existed in DSM-II, which had even abandoned the former DSM-I category of so-called "gross stress reaction," when it was published in 1968, the year of the Communist Tet Offensive in Vietnam.

Retrospect

There is currently a measure of consensus on the diagnosis and phenomenological description of PTSD, which is recognized as a specific syndrome in individuals who have experienced a major traumatic event. Most modern textbooks concur in describing this syndrome as comprising three groups of symptoms: (i) the recurrent and distressing reexperiencing of the event in dreams, thoughts, or flashbacks; (ii) emotional numbing and avoidance of stimuli reminiscent of the trauma; (iii) and a permanent state of increased arousal. The first symptoms of PTSD are often delayed and they are separated from the trauma by a latency period; however, once installed, the disorder tends to follow a chronic course and the symptoms do not abate with time. DSM-IV30 has the merit of clearly distinguishing PTSD, a chronic syndrome, from acute stress disorder, which is short-lived and appears soon after the trauma. We tend to abusively interpret the literature of previous decades as if today's diagnostic categories had always existed. However, a clear distinction between acute stress disorder and chronic PTSD is usually lacking in previous works. Also, there was little attempt to predict the risk of developing PTSD. Providing the trauma is severe enough, most individuals will go on to develop PTSD. However, one puzzling question is that many survivors seemingly do not develop symptoms even after a severe stressor.31 Likewise, the historical literature on PTSD offers few clues concerning effective treatment, once the symptoms have become chronic. The practice of forward treatment aiming to prevent the development of chronic disorders may have inspired today's psychological debriefing of disaster victims.

Desde el "corazón de soldado" y la "neurosis de guerra" al trastorno de estrés postraumático: una historia del trauma psíqui

La denominación de trastorno de estrés postraumático ha sido ampliamente reconocida desde su primera aparición en 1980 en la tercera edición del Manual Diagnóstico y Estadístico de los Trastornos Mentales (DSM-III) publicado por la Asociación Psiquiátrica Americana. Para la población general este diagnósti
se asocia con el desastroso legado de la Guerra de Vietnam. Una serie de conflictos bélicos anteriores han dado origen a otras denominaciones de esta patología como: "corazón de soldado", shock de la explosión y neurosis de guerra. Este último diagnóstico corresponde a la névrose de guerre y Kriegsneurose de la literature científica francesa y alemana respectivamente. Este artículo describe la forma en que las consecuencias –agudas y crónicas-del trauma psíquico hicieron su aparición en la literatura médica y cómo han evolucionado los conceptos diagnósticos a lo largo del tiempo.

Du shell shock et de la névrose de guerr à l'état de stress post-traumatique: une histoire de la psychotraumatologi

Depuis sa première apparition dans la troisième edition du Manuel Statistique et Diagnostique des Troubles Mentaux (DSM-III) publiée par l'American Psychiatric Association, la denomination "état de stress post-traumatique" est largement reconnue. Ce diagnostic évoque immédiatement la guerre du Vietnam et les séquelles qu'elle a engendrées. Lors de conflits plus anciens, d'autres denominations ont été utilisées telles que "coeur de soldat" "shell shock", ainsi que des termes "névrose de guerre" et "kriegsneurose" dans la littérature scientifique française et allemande. Cet article retrace l'historique de la description, dans la littérature médicale, des conséquences immédiates et chroniques de ces traumatismes psychologiques et l'évolution dans le temps des conceptions diagnostiques et thérapeutiques.

Afghanistan 2006

Having left Iraq the previous year, we found ourselves being the first squadron (18 Sqn B Flt) and Flight to return in 2006. In 2002, 27 Sqn Chinooks and crews were deployed with Royal Marines to aid in the search for Osama Bin Ladin and we know what happened to him eventually. Afghanistan is three times the size of the UK with half the population and with a huge mountainous area.

A new place and a different mindset and a different enemy. The British vacated Afghanistan to focus on Iraq in 2003 and so we left the area to other nationalities and a few of our Special Forces to oust Al Qaeda.

This time we had briefs, intelligence on the Taliban, we knew our tactics and aircraft, weapon systems like the back of or hands thanks to the time in Iraq. We also knew we would be given no quarter by the Taliban and on a pre-detachment brief, we were told not to except that all of us would come home alive.

What we didn't have, is knowledge of the land and operating around Helmand. Kandahar was already 3000 feet above sea level without climbing into the mountains and this would have consequences on engine performance and lift capability in the high areas or very hot conditions.

Mix them both, hot and high and you do have to complete the calculations for the performance ability of the aircraft. This would denote the weight we could carry and for how long and if we had to drop a load from being underslung in an emergency or understand that we would be going down in certain circumstances, like losing an engine.

We arrived at Kandahar to find that the Yanks and Canadians had been there for years. Bastion hadn't been built so we operated out of Kandahar airfield for the first year or so. Transiting from Kandahar to Helmand province took about 45 minutes by air and you would follow certain geographical features.

On route to Helmand, the desert leading to the border with Pakistan was on your left. It was a typical sandy, dune-based desert with not much plant life. The edge of the desert would then drop away to a flat valley floor for a few miles before it started to ascend towards the mountain range. The desert literally just stopped, like someone had put up an invisible wall and it had reached the side.

You could tell instantly this wasn't a place who gave two fucks about you whether you lived or died. Everywhere you flew, people just stopped and stared, didn't wave, raise hands but you were so close you could see their piercing light blue eyes just glare at you.

Kandahar being Pashtun (local Muslim tribe that has spread and who pride themselves on being one of the first people to adopt Islam 4th century AD) was a very pro-Taliban city. The Taliban had a lot of protection and friends there and it was ideally suited quite close to Pakistan as to offer the first city over the border.

The Canadians were responsible for that province and they took a heavy toll in and around Kandahar. The route around Kandahar was renamed IED Alley or Bomb Alley and unfortunately, many a Canadian soldier lost their lives or were seriously injured by these devices.

I attended a ramp ceremony for six Canadian soldiers who were killed by an IED in March 2007, and I wrote in my diary,

"Thousands turned out and if those 6 going upwards looked back down, they would have seen thousands of soldiers saluting their bravery."

Afghanistan was the Opium hub of the world and a significant amount came from the Helmand province and through Sangin. All these areas were controlled by the Taliban in some way and whatever your views on religious freedom, there was nothing free about fundamental Islam and 4th century ideals and cruelty in this day and age. Again poverty was rife and the threshold between living and starving was a close balanced thing.

Kandahar airfield was full of aircraft and a huge military base. It was very well set up, as many American bases are, and the accommodation and mess halls superb. We even got hardened accommodation from the yanks but they turfed us out eventually.

Sharing a room with the Det Co, Deputy Det Co, Senior crewman, etc, we had it very comfortable. Our new boss coming from the dark side (chinook role in supporting UK special forces) was asleep like we all were when there was a large explosion. Up he shot out of his scratcher and on went the lights,

"What was that?" he said.

"A rocket or shell," came the reply.

"We are under attack."

"Where should we go?" he asked.

"Back under your Kevlar duvet as there's nowhere to go." None of us moved, there were no shelters as such, they came later.

The next night we came under rocket or 155 shell fire again. This time, he sat bolt upright and none of us moved again, he soon got the idea that there wasn't anywhere to escape to, so went back to sleep.

Some days were kind of magical, the poppy harvest had finished and all the poppies would have flowered around April. There would be acres of poppies, thousands of acres near and around the province.

The colours were astounding but the fragrance was unbelievable. We would deliberately fly low level and over the fields, the perfume would fill the cab as if taking a shower in rose water.

Flying over the desert at dawn or early evening, the desert was an iridescent red, such changes of colour as the sun climbed or dipped from the horizon.

Several times, we had to resupply the American bases in the mountains at Forts Anaconda, Cobra and Taren Kout. The trips were adventurous as you would go past where previous battles had been fought.

During the winter months, these outposts would use donkeys for transport and we saw the stables with the pack animals feeding. It seemed strange that the most developed and largest military power ever on earth still had to rely on the basics to achieve the task. On the other hand, utilise what you have to achieve the aim.

The MERT was born in Afghanistan with the Chinook helicopter acting as an air ambulance and being utilised as the best asset to pick up the serious and not so seriously wounded.

It had the room for a four-person medical team with force protection and the ability to take multiple casualties. It was also used time and time again as an initial operating theatre as some wounded couldn't wait out the ride to hospital at Camp Bastion.

With all the kit and troops getting on and off every day, there was usually some good finds that had been left behind on the cab. We always did a sweep through if just a normal off-load and handed what we found to the ground asset or last person off, but if it was a tactical landing then, once the troops and kit were off, then it was ramp up and airborne ASAP.

One such find was a 9mm Browning pistol, standard issue for most until its replacement, the Glock 17. It had fallen through one of the zip pockets between the seats and as we approached Bastion, there was a call over the net to ask if someone had found the Colonel's pistol. It was returned to Garesk, the next serial to a most probably very relieved officer.

I, on the other hand, didn't have as much luck. Besides the aircraft being defended by flares and one port, one starboard M134 minigun and a ramp M60, we also carried our personal weapons, each crew member had a pistol and a rifle.

Rather than carry the rifle working on the cab, we as crewmen would secure the rifle near our crash seats. Ammunition, before being incorporated into the body armoured crew jacket, was in pouches alongside the weapon.

One particular day, we had loads of serials to the same place Garesk, just offloading and on loading troops. I believe there might have been a job on around Garesk which would explain the build-up. However, with a cab full of troops you have to keep your eyes peeled not just outside but inside also.

Many a time, soldiers have tried to walk off with our go-kits thinking it was someone's from their troop. This time, however, I do not doubt that the thieving git knew what he was doing. As we prepared to descend to low level, I went onto the ramp gun.

We tactically manoeuvred and landed without incident at FOB Rob near Garesk, ramp down, troops, out, ramp up and "clear above and behind" from the No 2 Crewman and off we went.

Once high level, I went to position myself at the left-hand bubble window when I noticed my pouches of ammunition had vanished. Since the pouches were clipped on to the seat netting, it would take some serious force to knock them off and there would be signs of damage.

No damage is seen, so I looked under the seat, around the cab and came to the conclusion that some thieving git from the last drop off had just pinched my four magazines and 120 rounds of 5.56.

Even with a call over the net to Garesk drew little concern, so I was left with the issue of replacing 120 rounds of 5.56 without getting in the shit. Letting off a round accidentally is called a negligent discharge and that incurred the penalty of your Op bonus taken away as a fine. What the hell would 120 rounds cost then? I'd be owing them money.

Well, sometimes it's not what you know but who and with two dozen Timmy Horton glazed doughnuts and a bit of an explanation I managed to acquire 120 rounds and four magazines.

The magazines were the hard part, the rounds, well most nationalities in theatre used 5.56 calibre and so I didn't lose my ass from that. Where I got them from and who, you would be surprised how helpful people are when you've rescued one of their own.

Talking about helping people, I was tasked to see the French Officer in charge of air movement in theatre for the French special forces (SF), he was in Kandahar. The SF troops were stationed at a place south of Kandahar called Spin Baldak in the Panjwai district about 1km from the Pakistan border and a good intercept point.

The Americans didn't have any assets available and if a big Op was going in over the next few days and nights assets were drawn from other duties. So, we were tasked to complete a drop of supplies for them. Talking to the French Officer, the local Int suggested it wasn't a good place to hang around and definitely not to shut down.

Two Chinooks were tasked to take equipment to a drop off point near to the base. It would take a bit off time to unload and the French were not keen on hanging around outside, they knew the area far better than we did and if the French SF were concerned then so should we be.

Everything was going to get delivered on pallets to the aircraft, but we didn't have a rolling floor like the fixed-wing has, so we made one up. Borrowing from other places, we cobbled together a makeshift roller conveyor, restraining with the use of P-Strops and with some Paracord to act as cut lines.

The idea being, we would descend, lower our speed to fast walking pace, lift the nose and cut the Para cord allowing gravity to push the pallets out with a push from ourselves.

We completed a dry run with an empty pallet, made up a plan and briefed both crews. On the day, we travelled only about 10 minutes to the site and set up for the run, coming in slow the ramp was dropped below the horizontal but not too much, the Para cords were cut after the restraints were removed and the pallets moved out.

Everything went smoothly and we landed as they wanted a person to return. These were big men, huge beards, broad and hard, like the ones you see carrying the axe at the front of the parade during Bastille day.

On return, I had to go to the French Officer for a debrief. He was chuffed, it worked very well and we got chatting about France. I mentioned that my parents lived there, but got a shrug of impudence.

However, he did offer me a bottle of red and a slice of cheese for my effort. I politely turned it down as I said it was a Flight effort and I couldn't sit there enjoying this with only a couple of people.

How could he refuse, so he gave me a case of red wine and two blocks of cheeses, one hard and one soft, obviously all from France. Like many continental countries, troops still get an allowance of alcohol with their main meals.

After the evening prayers with the boss at 1830, the flight was invited to where I had my scratcher (bed) and the disbelief that I had wangled booze and cheese off the French.

While in Iraq we could get away with the occasional libation, here in Afghanistan it was a no-no, you never knew what you were doing next or when you had to get up, it wasn't worth it professionally.

However, that night we got the all clear and we went from happy, chirpy people to quite pissed with two glasses of wine. It was one of those moments, the impromptu ones, party in the kitchen type that turns into gold dust and was a great blowout for us all.

We moved to Bastion the following detachment and what started as a small tented town reached huge proportions later on. I have to say the food was amazing and the military chefs had been replaced with Sri Lankan civilians, not only cheaper to hire but the curries were exceptional.

It had taken years but what a way to dine. The facilities had taken on the same style as the Americans with coffee houses and fast-food joints. The shopping experiences were never going to match the American BX system but better than they had ever been before.

Bastion was in the middle of no-where and as such, we didn't come under mortar or rocket fire, a few were discovered being assembled but were taken care of. There was. however, an assault with suicide Taliban that blew up a huge lorry bomb at the fence line allowing entry to the base.

They destroyed several American harrier aircraft, killed two and injured 17 soldiers. All but one of the 15 fighters was killed with the response from the 51 Sqn RAF Regiment Force Protection taking the fight to the enemy. We still felt relatively safe at Bastion, it wasn't the threat of the Taliban, it was the spies inside the base that were the problem.

Having local inhabitants work on building projects allowed them access to view the inside of the base. Every time they entered or exited the station, they were searched and many a time, plans, drawings, numbers, etc were written down and hidden on them were found.

They even managed mobile phones and videoed locations; these were all part of reconnaissance techniques for the Taliban. Usually, they just forced their way into villages and demanded answers, we were told of a village elder who was questioned by the Taliban, they didn't like the answer they got so they shot his eight-year-old grandson as punishment, draconian and evil.

All over Afghanistan, there are stories of atrocities which these and other Islamic extremists meet out because of the most unbelievable of reasons, no beard or not long enough, listened to music, wore makeup, showed their hairline (females), walking without a male relative escort (female), the list goes on.

To be honest, I don't understand religion, on the one hand, those people that have the belief are so lucky to find something so rewarding and giving and know they have faith to overcome most of life's difficulties. They look at the good to do and adopt and peaceful existence helping fellow humans.

On the other, it's used as a shackle to enforce and control, making life intolerable and miserable, not allowing freedom (As through the eyes of a westerner) and discipline enforced to ensure capitulation.

My mother was from the highlands of Scotland was brought up a Catholic and taught by nuns in the Convent School in the thirties and forties, discipline was strict and many a mistake was met with physical violence.

Even with her death, she had to repent to meet her maker, born a sinner and forever trying to become good enough to enter God's Kingdom, eternal life of not being good enough.

On the one hand, it tells of being kind to your fellow man and doing good deeds and on the other, you'll never do enough to be free from the stigma of being a sinner and shamed off the guilt. FUCK OFF!

I believe the two most misguided and most responsible elements that have caused the most misery, atrocities and death in the world for thousands of years are religion and greed. Both have caused tens, if not hundreds of millions of deaths.

One believes it is the most righteous and divine, thereby allowing itself to do whatever it takes (and it doesn't matter which one you take as your religion) and the other doesn't take responsibility for its actions but survives on the selling of the idea that is impossible for 95% of the people.

Back to reality!

Bastion was a busy area and a very busy airfield. It was officially the busiest helicopter site in the world. It had a fantastic hospital run by medical teams from all three services and civilian doctors, surgeons and nursing staff that would don a uniform just to supply help to us but I think a great way for them to learn first-hand at these types of injuries.

Night flying one night, we as the crew, had dropped off our task and were returning to Bastion when in the distance we saw a very bright, what only can be described as an afterburner. It was called to the front and mentioned that fast air was low in our 9 o'clock, several miles away.

After a few seconds, it came back from the cockpit that it wasn't fast air as it was travelling far too fast. What we were seeing was a meteor with its tail ignited due to the speed through the air.

It glowed for a long time as if parallel but we had to turn away towards our destination, I've always wondered what that meteor would have looked like and its size.

Having not been in theatre for a few years it was a culture shock returning in 2011 with the Merlins. The Area of Operations (AO) had shrunk massively but the pre-briefs before even being allowed to deploy out of the wire were swept up.

The basic battlefield first aid was brilliant, as were so many other briefs about the Taliban, latest Int, etc. This is what should have been happening so many years ago at the start of the conflict and Iraq.

As the AO had shrunk that meant the Taliban had fewer targets against the allies and so the action increased against those bases. The Afghan National Army (ANA) who were taking over these bases were getting a pasting.

The Afghan National Police (ANP) were also being infiltrated and you couldn't rely on information not being passed to the enemy or even posts being manned when something was due to go on.

At the beginning of July 2011, the Americans were again on the receiving end and a crewman fell out of one of the V22s Osprey airborne and hit the deck from 200 feet. Two Pedro's were shot through the legs on the helicopter going to rescue someone.

Dust storms were frequent and aggressive making flying difficult, it would look like you were flying through a goldfish bowl and sometimes couldn't discern sky from the ground.

The insurgents would use this opportunity of cover to plant IEDs and launch attacks. One group were seen planting IEDs 100m from a Control Point (CP), they got a Javelin missile up their chuff that sorted them out.

The Americans wouldn't hesitate in opening fire and we were coming into land at an American base when we saw a dicker talking into a mobile pointing at the site. We passed the info on and the Americans had the ability to listen in to the chat, he didn't say a lot a few minutes later as a ground call sign took him out.

The ANA and ANP while being mentored by the British and Americans and most probably other nationalities were still filled with spies and many occasions those spies when they had an opportunity turned, the very weapons they were being trained with, on to their teachers.

Diary

18 July: soldier hit by IED dies on Chinook. ANP CP overran by Taliban several dead.

4 coordinated attacks on CPs within 40 minutes.

21 July: Two more double amputees today.

Transit to Karnikar lots of 105-mm and 155-mm shells leaving the camp as we depart.

Listening to four radios on the cab and one call sign left his live, listened to the firefight and someone getting shot.

22 July: Three separate incidents of insurgents planting bombs, all got whacked by helicopters.

23 July: Hospital move of civilians from Bastion to Lashkah Gar to make space for more wounded soldiers.

Picked up an attack dog but wouldn't stop pissing next to and on the ramp, the dog that is. I couldn't give it a bollocking as it was evil. The heavily laden troops kept slipping on the ramp and falling over.

Passed accident on route 1 where a minibus had hit a lorry or other way around, bodies scattered around like fallen debris and hanging out of the windows.

24 July: News of two British Insurgents picked up near the border with Iran.

Picked up four detainees caught with RPG warheads. Lots of artillery going into the green zone from our guns.

31 July: Taliban trying to destabilise Geroa, in Lashkah Gar. A bomb hit a bus injuring 18 mainly women and children.

Lashkah Gar suicide bomber they think was a boy, drove a roller into a truck, 10 KIA, 16 injured.

I had to pick up six coffins of the Afghan police, lots of bodily fluids escaping into the aircraft, trying to come up with a plan to sort out.

Throughout the summer months, the British Apaches had been having a lot of success with insurgents and in one week in July had KIA 27 of them. Objective Parker destroyed while driving his car.

5 Aug: IED, one Brit head injuries. 8 Insurgents KIA, 3 IEDS, Merlin hit.

9 Americans Casevac to Bastion as IED.

7 Aug: Insurgents are getting at locals by kidnapping, burning alive and killing village elders. US Chinook hit on the ground with RPG, 31 Seals, 4 crew, 7 Afghans and 1 other all perished. Several attacks on Patrol Bases (PBS) with underslung grenade launchers and small arms fire. Possible triple-A in theatre and Dushka.

9 Aug: It seems strange to watch the riots in London whilst out here. The suggestion of moving the decompression site from Cyprus to a London pub, fill it with Bootnecks (Royal Marines) and let them onto the street.

10 Aug: J2 Int, Insurgents have Russian sniper rifles with laser targeting. They believe that is hat has caused so much trouble with the American helicopters.

Watched Objective Parker and Beefcake being splashed by Apache, over 80 IED players KIA this year in our AO.

13 Aug: Americans lose 60 men this month in Afghanistan.

17 Aug: Had a very interesting and long chat with an old friend now an Apache pilot. We discussed standards, discipline, the effects of our actions in Afghanistan and the neutralisation of emotions in killing people.

His ability to brush off or show any emotion when talking about 'Killed three people before breakfast yesterday and two before lunch today' and the nature of desensitisation. To what he has had to complete shows the impact of what four tours on Apache does in Afghanistan.

The British Apaches tally of KIA in July are mostly foreign fighters. Very few are locals anymore which means Pakistan and the tentacles from ISI are still strong.

18 Aug: 4.15 tonnes of homemade explosive (HME) captured in operation. Big find denying enemy IED explosives, expect strong connectivity increase as a show of force from insurgents.

31 Aug: Several IEDs throughout AO. Two at south Lashkah Gah, one at CP 5 KIA, one by bank queue with locals, lots of children injured.

Eve of Eid has gone and waiting for the final big one before the foreign fighters depart over the mountains pre-winter and melt across the borders.

New crews in theatre to take over, I ensured all of my crewmen have departed theatre as quickly as possible, just the OC, Dep OC and me left. Had an incident a few weeks ago and still feeling the pain (see Ground 1—Helicopter 0), compared with others, its slight and I'm still here.

That was my last helicopter flight in Afghanistan and my life so far, but I went on to return in 2013 with the Air Transport Air Bridge on the now-defunct Tri-Star aircraft. I only lasted four months, and then my world turned upside down and inside out.

I think by the end, I had burnt out, strung out and was completely fed up with these going no-where detachments. By the end of Iraq, we had slipped away at the dead of the night pulling out of southern parts and as I look at Iraq now in 2019, what's changed for the positive?

A country while proud, is severely split religiously and the continual infighting between factions and government and those spindly fingers from aggressive neighbours.

I look at Afghanistan now and we are still deploying troops there to shore up a government that cost over a trillion dollars to help maintain some sort of governance. 375 American helicopters were downed up to the summer of 2009 with 70 being downed by hostile fire.

These numbers do not include any other nation or past 2009, the numbers are massive but also point at the aggressiveness of the environment. To lose 305 helicopters to non-hostile action says a lot of the hostile terrain and may shine a light on the type of flying and training and acceptance of risk they take compared to other nationalities.

To date, there are still reports of killings and over-runs of positions and checkpoints and hundreds being killed by the Taliban.

When you look at both Iraq and Afghanistan, what do you know about these countries? Realistically, due to media coverage a hell of a lot and more than you would otherwise. For several years, it maintained the news daily or weekly with reports of gains and changing landscapes. Did we change that much or was Iraq 2003 a boy trying to complete his father's mission from 13 years previously.

Why these two countries, compared to the plethora of others suffering the same religious bigotry and cruelness dished out regularly through villages raised to the ground. Do people really know the numbers of countries that are at war or conflict because of religion, especially Islam?

Look at the African continent and the dozens of countries that are still seeing teenagers with no kit as such just a weapon and told to go and fight and end up just being thrown into graves or the sea. I don't think we understand the fate of many others in different countries until it impacts our own or costs us money.

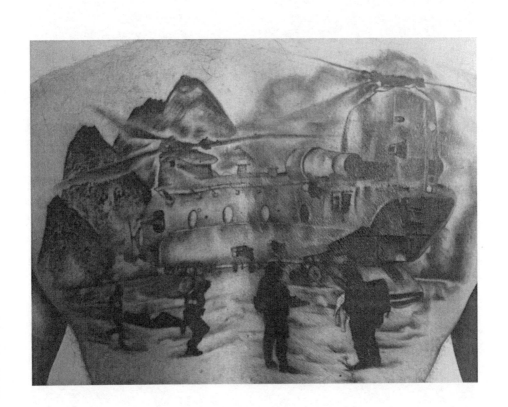

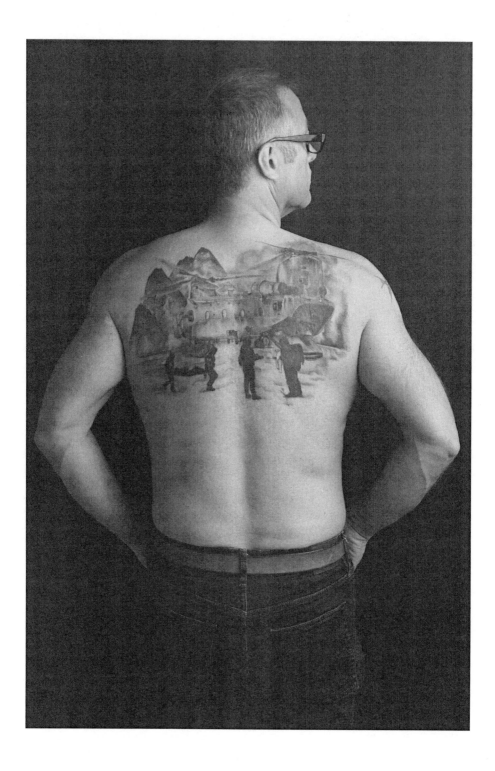

My Tipping Point

What I am about to write about, would not have been possible several months before, as even the act of recalling or remembering would have been too much to bear.

The process that has enabled me to get this far is down to the excellent work Veterans Mental Health Complex Treatment Service. This has started in my ability to live with those events that have had a cataclysmic effect on me.

The Girl in the White Dress

This was my second tour of Afghanistan and my tenth overall in Theatre of Operations (TORs). Helmand was starting to get busier in terms of threats and the Taliban more focussed on dislodging the enemy.

I had been attached to another Chinook Squadrons manpower for their detachment to Helmand due to a shortage. I was in date a majority of my theatre currencies only having returned a couple of months previously, it made sense to add me to their nominal role. We all, from time to time, had to take that extra burden but it never seemed to be felt as such.

I was in my detachment cycle of activity being on the Casevac (Casualty Evacuation) helicopter crew or MERT cab. The other two cycles being normal daily tasking and Deliberate Operations.

The crew consisted of two crewmen and two pilots. Onboard we had a dedicated MERT unit (Medical Emergency Response Team) which consisted of a doctor, anaesthetist, paramedic and nurse. Each role had their specific tasks but it was amazing to watch such synergy in all their actions in preserving life that hung so delicately, sometimes, in the balance.

There was also a team of eight infantry soldiers that rotated for a week on the aircraft to act as a protection party when the Chinook landed often in very hostile territory.

We were all lazing in the tent next to the flight line (this allowed for the crew and ground crew, MERT, etc to run to the helicopter and get airborne in the quickest possible time) when the phone rang.

The call went up and we raced to the aircraft with the captain going to operations (Ops) to ascertain the nature of the task, location, how and what type of casualties, threat and escort if required.

Our usual escort was an Apache helicopter with their impressive arsenal of weapons. If it was deemed the threat was significant or the TIC (Troops in Contact) was still ongoing, then we may have received two Apache escorts.

Having an asset such as an airborne ambulance albeit with two miniguns and a ramp M60 machine gun did provide that essential golden hour to get the casualties to a full surgical hospital.

The MERT, was able to, if it came to it, operate on the aircraft to preserve life. I have witnessed casualties, unfortunately, losing their life signs only to be brought back by the work of the MERT.

As crew operating on the Casevac aircraft, that could be the difference between getting a casualty to hospital and picking up a body, we held in no doubt the significance of our task.

There had been instances when helicopters had been banned from landing at certain Landing sites (LS) due to the ferocity of the battle going on, however, the Casevac aircraft, with help from the Apaches, never refused a request for a Tier 1 casualty that I know of.

There was a crew with a Chinook that sustained so much battle damage they had to take the Chinook back to base for them only to transfer all their kit onto another Chinook to go and retrieve the casualty.

There were British Chinooks that sustained so much damage with RPG's and small arms fire they have landed with the entire cabin roof on fire but that's another story from another crew.

With the Casevac aircraft, all personal kit, weapons, medical equipment and even the pre-flight walk around have been stowed or completed before we get a call. It is a question of getting on the helicopter and starting up and getting airborne as soon as possible waiting for the captain to brief us on the task on the transit.

Today, we were informed that there had been a Taliban land mine strike on a tractor. For us, it didn't sound too bad, a casualty or two from the local populous and not one of our own as in a soldier from any allied country. Sounds blasé, maybe cruel, but it was a fact of life.

The landing site was very near the green zone and as such within range of mortar and small arms/machine guns.

We identified the landing area due to popped smoke from the ground call sign and proceeded to descend and carry out a dust landing approach. The aircraft came to a halt and the captain gave the 'clear ramp' and the soldiers and MERT team exited towards the ground troops and casualties.

We, on the aircraft, kept an eye out for potential enemy activity, the situation on the ground and prep for the return leg. Time was ticking by and the more time spent on the ground near an enemy location, the more time the enemy had to prepare a strike. It also crosses your mind that this may be a 'come on' and was planned to lure troops and the Helicopter into a pre-planned assault.

The chatter on the airwaves, Taliban FM, always talks of downing a helicopter and sometimes on return and the subsequent debrief, the Taliban were nearly ready to engage with the enemy, us.

Some assets (British) were unlucky and did get hit, some with small arms (SA), heavy machine gun (HMG) and even rocket-propelled grenades (RPG). Other allied assets took a heavier toll with recoiled rifles rounds going through the cockpit and the Chinook falling from the sky.

Our front end (Pilots) were getting edgy as it was taking longer than it should. One of the soldiers from the protection party came back on board and explained that a family of nine had been hit, with the trailer carrying the family taking the brunt, two were in very serious condition.

That shifted the focus on the cab and we knew that we had to move fast on the return leg. The MERT four rushed on board with two stretchers and some soldiers and started working on the two seriously injured. It was fast and frantic work but the rest of the casualties were still to follow.

The captain asked me to get things moving and I came off the harness to help collect the casualties as there were not enough troops to bring everyone on board.

The grandmother and mother walked on board and sat near the stretchers but were in total silence. Other injured starting to arrive with an approximately 14/15-year-old boy being given a shoulder to allow him to limp on board as his ankle had been ripped apart with shrapnel.

It now wasn't the issue of enemy activity but getting the wounded to hospital. I jumped off the ramp turned left and bumped directly into a soldier carrying a bundle of clothes, it was a white dress, it was an infant with black hair.

The soldier held out his arms for me to take the girl. The bundle didn't move and the head was limp with eyes closed. The dress was a brown dusty colour but something else in that fraction of a second hit me.

The dress was ripped, torn, shredded and it had blood on it. I froze, in that instant, it could have been 2 seconds, 20 seconds, 200 seconds, the soldier said, "here, take her" and my arms went out and I took the little girl. I can honestly say that this, rather than at any other, time in my life, I totally lost all ability to function.

Maybe it was the straw that broke the camel's back, maybe it was because I had a son that was the same age, maybe it was a culmination of all that I had witnessed before and this time my mind stopped working. I remember taking the girl into the cabin and was trying to find someone to take her from me, I didn't want to keep holding her, I didn't know what to do.

What seemed like a long time, I gave the girl to one of the onboard infantry soldiers. We got airborne and that means I must have got everybody on board, lifted the ramp and positioned myself for take-off by the ramp gun.

I cannot recall much of the details now, but remember that I was sitting on the ramp looking at the scene going on in front of me unfold, which tells me we must have climbed to height and I was off the ramp gun.

All I can recall is the total loss of functioning state, in my mind I was asking myself,

'What could I have done, what should I have done, why didn't I do anything'.

I was in shock and I didn't have the resources to help me get out of it or deal with it. I felt inadequate and that self-belief I had, we have, as Aircrew left me.

As Crewman (that includes women also, who happen to be extremely efficient in the Crewman role), we pride ourselves at delivering what our users require and more often than not delivering more due to the lack of knowledge by the user units.

We have a phenomenal asset with the Chinook and mix that with an experienced crew, there are not many places or tasks we cannot achieve.

I had just been dumped on my ass and I knew it was going to affect me, we rallied and headed for Lashkah Gar where we radioed ahead for ground support to help us with these casualties.

The HQ had rallied the ground forces and medical teams, there were people everywhere to meet us with stretchers. The most serious were offloaded and we helped with the rest. I noticed the teen lad hopping to join his family so I picked him up and carried him to a stretcher.

His ankle was a right mess but like the majority of Afghan casualties, not a peep or a cry from any of them. He was so light, he must have only weighed about six stone, I could have picked him up with one hand.

With all the casualties offloaded, we had all the MERT and infantry return to the aircraft. On the way back to Kandahar (Bastion was still being built, and consisted of two 20x20 metre concrete squares, within a couple of years it was the size of Reading) I was very quiet, ASBO the other Crewman that day asked if everything was alright and I gave him a thumbs up but he knew I wasn't in a good place.

ASBO was an enormously square-shouldered Welsh guy who had the ability to grin through everything, he always had a way of making people smile. I believe he went onto Search and Rescue duties post Chinook.

When we returned to Kandahar as always post flight, you had to reset the cab exactly how you found it. I can't remember if we were taken off the Casevac line or it was crew change time but I found myself sitting outside our accommodation contemplating what had happened.

ASBO sat the other side of the table and asked if everything was alright and I admit I was going to tell him how I felt but the pilots turned up and on their way passed asked,

"You're Ok, aren't you, Simon?" I look back at that moment and realise it was then that everything was locked away. I turned and said,

"Yeah, I'm OK." That was the instant I shut everything out and didn't process that memory or even acknowledge it, it was a put up and shut up and get on with the job moment.

Inside I was still struggling with the aspect that I didn't have what it took to achieve the mission or realistically help the girl. I felt so inadequate through lack of ability, I couldn't help her as I didn't know what to do and that hit home hard.

This event more than others would catch up with me several years down the line but for now, it was work as usual unless kids were involved, which unfortunately, the next two weeks were.

I think this was the start of my downfall but I didn't grip or understand anything about it. I felt changed to the point of feeling dirty, I felt that it was visible to others even though I didn't know what I was showing. What do I say, who do I go to?

If I go to the medical centre, they will surely stop me flying. There is enough shortage on the Chinook fleet that crewmen are taken from other flights to fill gaps in the operational roulement, you don't want to be another desk worker. More to the point, you don't want to lose your flying pay.

At one point, a close mate called Andy W took me aside and drove me around to the other side of the airfield. We had a chat, but I couldn't find the right message, question, answer, I just didn't know what was happening to me.

A few years down the line, that man came to me and we did the reverse. Through my counsellor, I now see where things started to get unbalanced for me and what effect it has had short, medium and ultimately long term. Now, it's about deciphering those incidents and allowing the brain to process those traumas to allow you to live with them.

They will never go away; they just get dealt with by a different method. Have I been damaged, yeah, for far too long I kept things hidden and just locked away and that storage over time became fuller and fuller and then just left, ignored.

Sometimes, it would cause a reaction, others an emotional outburst, eventually, it would make me quite ill. The first step of recovery is accepting there is something wrong, the second is being ready to deal with it and that can be years apart.

A Bit of a Heavy Landing

I awoke this day not knowing this would be my last helicopter flight in the RAF. I was on my fourth tour of Afghanistan but with the Merlin helicopter for this detachment which at the time was based at RAF Benson in Oxfordshire.

Today was a routine tasking day from an ever-decreasing Area of Operations (AO). There were roughly four main Forward Operating Bases (FOBs) left and a few desert landing areas. I know I had been away for a few years but this was a shock to see us operating in a bit of a back yard in Helmand.

At the beginning of 2006, the deployed forces in Helmand province operated around a small part of Helmand and Kandahar province. As the size of the force grew along with the infrastructure then, so did the footprint of the British presence.

With the history of Sangin, Gereshk, Kajaki, Now Zad, Musa Qala, 2 Victoria Crosses and a multitude of films showing the violence and frustration of the situation in Helmand and Afghanistan, along with all the social media, I found myself again operating in Helmand in 2011.

It had changed dramatically from the aspect of where we went and what we had control of, as in, ground and FOBs, so reduced from 2007 onwards, I knew. Tasking was much the same with the usual internal loads, troops and sometimes underslung loads (USLs).

We had departed first light and continued throughout the day on tasking around the area. To allow a greater payload at our operating height, high temperatures and greater engine performance, we usually took on less fuel. This was now a matter of course and at the end of the tasking day, we would refuel up to 2,000 kg for the next tasking crew or day.

This is where we were when another Merlin helicopter taxied behind us at the refuelling spot. We had finished tasking for the day and were due to shut down at around 17:45/18:00.

One of the crewmen from the second cab came over to the ramp and handed us a brown envelope. Inside was some information about grid references and an Aerial picture, we had no idea what it was about and explained to the visiting crewman that we had finished tasking.

He explained back that we have been re-tasked and also to brief his crew on what the task was. He mentioned that we had attended the early morning brief with the Chinook and Lynx crews on this task.

The discussion back and forward took some time to decipher but we had indeed been re-tasked but had asked the question at the early morning brief that if it was a Chinook task why were we attending. It wasn't on our tasking serial sheet for the day and as such, we the Merlin crew, were dismissed from the necessity of a brief.

We now found ourselves quickly reading over the plan, it was to insert two four-man teams. Each team had a sniper and sharpshooter element to it and each Merlin was to drop off their team and supplies with a Lynx helicopter from the British Army providing the necessary overhead protection (Mutual Support).

It was also coming to the end of the day and like a lot of countries closer to the equator than Britain, night falls quickly whatever time it arrives. We had no night vision goggles on board the aircraft and we discussed shutting down and re-planning for a night insert.

It would take another couple of hours with transport, kitting and replanning with maps, so we as a crew agreed to press ahead and continue on task straight away before it got dark.

We asked the other crew to take lead as they had, we believed more time to look at the task and the landing area. As we found out later, they had as much idea as us on the task as they were informed that we had received the brief.

When the Crew Resource Management (CRM) teams discuss all the cheeses coming into line, it means the cheese with holes in it that when you add all the incorrect decisions, made you can see right through several slices, this was definitely one of those moments.

The idea is, if you take one of those decisions away then you most probably would have solid cheese and as such, break that decision chain to potential disaster. When major accidents happen (when an aircraft crashes, it's usually a major accident), there is usually a series of events that led up to the accident.

If you ever watched *Chernobyl*, the TV three-parter about the lead up causes to Chernobyl's inevitable explosion and the decisions made that led it, you would get the idea. Principally, every decision has a consequence, when those decisions take you in the wrong direction, it leads you onto the next event, closer or finally to disaster.

When Aircrew are trained, we are taught about CRM and the need to speak up in an event that could likely or may lead to an unsatisfactory outcome. Even a chat amongst the crew can have the effect of mitigating that risk because it's been aired and is now known about. It also allows the crew to be aware of future decisions and their potential effect on the situation.

Where we had to set the teams down was in the middle of a very dusty middle of no-where land (not that we knew at the time) and a regular Taliban working area. The first cab completed the necessary checks and went into land.

What we saw from our standoff position was a very, very, dusty approach and landing. There wasn't much wind and so the cloud just hung around the area and climbed hundreds of feet into the air because of the downwash produced from the landing.

It was getting darker but still workable and would have been too bright for goggles and they would have backed down (the term used when a bright light enters the NVGs tube and distorts the image to the point of shutting down the goggles for a few seconds).

We had called for smoke and we approached according to Desert Standard Operating Procedure (SOPs) with me positioned on the ramp. As we descended, calls were made from positions from the crew whether, "100ft, 100knts", "in the gate" "Dust cloud building," etc.

We called for smoke a second time, and then we spotted the smoke from the ground indicating where we were to land but it was a late spot. I was at the time positioned on the ramp on the starboard side (right) and looking out of the rear of the aircraft and also scanning ahead around the side briefing on the approach of the dust cloud and the track ahead if I saw something not mentioned (looking for signs of incline or hazards).

There was a comment from the front or the No1 Crewman mentioning a vehicle tracks ahead. We all spotted them and they looked like a good indicator that it was a level surface. The light was fading but it gave us, as a crew, an indicator. We were wrong, we had just misread or our brains didn't compute the tracks correctly.

We were short finals to land and I had just pulled my head into the ramp area when there was a loud noise as the aircraft hit the deck. I shot forward at a great speed, I was airborne and going through the cabin when I suddenly came to a halt and fell on two of the Army troops we were carrying.

It took me some time to reorganise my brain (a couple of seconds). I had been catapulted from the ramp and my harness had stopped my flight. I was very lucky, very, very lucky, two seconds earlier and I would have been probably decapitated by the side of the aircraft.

First thought or instant thought was, we had been hit by the enemy. Then I started hearing the crew talk, I lost my hearing for a few seconds as I didn't hear the 'Mayday' calls go out to Ops. The cab was shaking and making a lot of bad noises, those noises you hear in a crash and know that isn't going to buff out, and we were on the ground but still unsure what had happened.

I heard the crew talking about a tail rotor strike, so I immediately got up from my position lying across the army (not comfortable, far too bulky) and went to the ramp area. The handling pilot was fighting with the controls to keep the aircraft stable as much as a shaking helicopter can be.

The tail rotor was about 8 inches off the ground and still turning fast with no signs of damage. The front end still discussed about a tail strike and I passed on the information that there was no sign of a strike on the ground, the tail rotor was spinning true and there was no unnatural noise coming from the tail rotor or gearbox.

What was mentioned was that the aircraft was 14 degrees nose up on a compound slope. The limit is 8 degrees, now we started to understand why we were in this position, we had banged into a bit of a hillside.

We discussed getting airborne as we couldn't stay there and we would start attracting the Taliban. The handling pilot tried to lift but the tail dipped and I called "height is good." We couldn't afford for the tail to dip, if it did, the tail would strike and we would possibly end up rolling down that slope we were on.

The Captain and Co-pilot discussed their plan and we lifted successfully into the hover. The Captain was handling and the Co-Pilot was constantly, softly providing information to the pilot. The pilot was working hard to control the aircraft and the heightened sense of what had happened, I am sure, made everyone a bit tunnel-visioned.

While the cab was still shaking and making a racket, it was a considerably lot less than when we were on the ground. We limped away and stayed low level and at low speed, we had no idea how damaged the cab was or if we would have to land immediately.

The troops on the aircraft were briefed on the incident and it was mentioned we may have to abandon the aircraft. So there were four RAF crew contemplating their demise in the hands of the Taliban and four army troops who now think they are going to get into a bit of a fight. I let you guess who was enjoying the experience more by the grins on their faces.

We heard over the radio that an Apache was scrambled and the American Pedro's had changed direction to come and help us. The Pedro's are a specialist unit that has the most experienced rescue personnel in the world. These men can parachute high or low level, trek over long mountainous areas, dive to perform submarine rescues, these guys go anywhere and rescue anything.

The second Merlin and Lynx, already in the know, followed us until we found a large walled compound about 12 miles away, it was the Afghanistan Police Training Head Quarters. We crossed the wall, moved forward to allow the other Merlin in and shut down.

We started to unload the cab, for some reason, as if we were going to re-supply the other cab and continue with the task. I didn't get the necessity that we had to go to the No 2 Merlin as they were short on fuel. Both of the crewmen on our cab did have the sense to unload the aircraft machine guns and take the barrels off the guns and hide them.

We ran on board the other Merlin and all of us just sat there in a total state of shock, we didn't say anything and didn't acknowledge anything. Once we got to Bastion, the aircraft was unloaded at the passenger point and I believe we were offloaded and our weapons were taken from us. We were told to get in a vehicle and even our kit didn't come with us, we were told to leave everything.

We entered the Merlin engineering area where we just sat and I think we were in a bit of delayed shock. I am sure we started talking about the incident and eventually, someone turned up and said we had to be separated.

We were asked to individually write down how the incident happened and not to cross-reference from each other. These statements were taken away and we were still just sitting around but not able to confer with anyone.

We were taken to see the Commander British Helicopter Forces Afghanistan. He was a very experienced helicopter pilot from the Royal Navy who first asked if we were ok. The front end were, the No 1 Crewman was as he said:

"I was pushed into the avionics cupboard but OK."

I was honest and said my back was playing up a bit but generally workable. Little did I know that several months down the line at Headley Court, a Brigadier

162

doctor would inform me the heavy landing had herniated two discs in my lower back and the snap of the harness reaching its length caused two in my neck to herniate as my head whipped forward then back.

The Helicopter Commander said he had already talked to our Squadron Commander (Wing Commander) and the Joint Helicopter Command Commander (2-star General from one of the services) in the UK. He reassured us that everything was ok and it wasn't our fault.

We listened but were still unsure of the reason why this path was being taken. The Commander was very honest and informed us that he had requested us to complete the task as the Chinook was called away for other duties.

The Commander having taken over the duties of the Operations Officer (OpsO) in the Operations room while the OpsO went for dinner had presumed we had been in the brief in the morning and wasn't updated otherwise.

The reasons why these 8 troops had to get to where they were going was important and decisions are made by far higher and more informed people than myself. The Commander made the decision and we followed the order but it was all the events that lead to this.

Yes, we missed the brief but we were experienced Aircrew that had the training to land in and on most surfaces whether sand, rough terrain, snow, mountain tops, ridges and ships, day or night, etc. Yes, we took on the task but preferable to land in the middle of the desert in the day than at night with no references.

Yes, we went without NVGs as to stop and get them would have taken us into night time landings. Yes, we thought the surface was flat, at that time, flying at that level with the sun going down and no visible references on the ground, we all thought it flat. The light level definitely played with our understanding of the land.

And yes, we landed near the smoke, unfortunately, as we found out the troops on the ground popped smoke when we first asked. What we didn't know was, it was hidden behind the previous dust cloud and had drifted down the slope for 40 seconds.

When we asked for a second smoke, what we saw was the first smoke appearing and it was called 'sighted'. That smoke was now descending, down the slope, we had no idea, was there.

There is no blame here, it was an unfortunate set of events that led to the aircraft being abandoned. What I did mention to the British Helicopter

163

Commander was that the two front enders or captain and co-pilot were so professional in their approach to resolving the issue and understanding the consequences of certain actions that they both deserved a big pat on the back.

The CRM at the front was exceptional with the non-handling pilot providing all the necessary information and dealing with the calls to Operations and the No 2 aircraft even after what had happened in a perfect, stable, approachable manner.

The handling pilot was pivotal in getting us airborne without dipping that tail a few inches and as such, the cab having a tail strike and at least tipping over if not descending towards the bottom of the slope. Yes, we all had fucked up, it happened but credit where credits due.

It took the engineers three weeks to fix that Category 1 damaged aircraft and the biggest crane in Afghanistan at that time, that took some getting hold of and transporting to the scene.

At home as in RAF Benson, word had already got around about the little heavy landing as an assessment of parts was required and that list went back to the UK. What happened next just shows how quickly nonsense can overlap reality.

An Op Minimise was called, this is a procedure where all lines to the UK whether phone or email is halted. The reason is, someone from the UK has been severely injured or even killed. Rather than some family members finding out about the loss of life or life-changing news on TV or worse from a neighbour, it is completed with as much dignity and purpose to support the family and allow them to know before anybody else does.

It allows those mechanisms to be put in place before it gets spread across the news. This Op Minimise, I believe, was called for such an event with British soldiers wounded in a blast. What happened at Benson was putting two and two together (Op Minimise and a list of spares for a Merlin) and come up with 125.

We heard, when we got back, that the gossip going around the married patch was one Crewman was dead and a pilot severely injured. That spread like wildfire and the bosses had to nip that in the bud before it started getting to the families of deployed personnel.

My wife had her parents over at our house when she received a call,

"Hello is that Mrs Richardson, it's 78 Sqn here from RAF Benson."

"Oh hello there," says the wife.

"Now, nobody has been killed or seriously injured," came next.

Mmmm, if my wife wasn't sure what was going on, she knew there was something up now.

It did all get resolved and apart from my back, all the crews on our detachment got home, just a lot lighter and thinner.

Sangin Resupply

In one of those odd moments in time, a normal tasking trip from early morning turned into the most colourful display of firepower I had been involved with.

We were up at the usual time of 03:30 local to get airborne first light around 05:30 to start the days tasking. This would allow us the cool temperatures of the morning to pick up and deliver heavy loads if required and utilise the entire sunlight of the day.

There was a two-ship into Lashkaghar with the first cab taking in an ISO container. This made them very vulnerable at low speeds with a great 8-9 tonne metal box hanging underneath. The rest of the sorties were troops and kit to and from various locations around the province.

We finished and returned after refuelling to Bastion at around 18:00. We knew there would be an operation to resupply Sangin and it was to be completed by three chinooks late at night around 23:00 hrs. Sangin was controlled by the Taliban and the operation which was destined for a later date, hadn't cleared the area yet.

To get in and out of Sangin District Centre (DC) was a feat in itself and the tactics utilised changed every time. This is not the place to spill the beans on what was done to counter the threat and how every trip was planned. This is one trip I flew on and was overwhelmed with wonderment with the entire experience.

I rushed from the day aircraft into the Helicopter Operations briefing tent and gently squeezed myself around the room to the other side of the table where I spotted a captain from one of the chinooks that would be going. Sidling up to him, I got a nod and then I heard,

"Anybody from the day crews here?" I put my hand up and this pilot said:

"I'll take Simon, I will brief him on the plan and he will operate on the third gun." This pilot was regarded by all as very skilful and he also worked well with the crew, always having time to listen and lead his crews. He went onto become the first RAF Apache pilot and 2 i/c of that Army Apache Squadron.

This was a brilliant tactic as good consideration was being given to the fact that I would have run out of crew hours. I was going to operate the port (Left) side minigun (the M134) and not operate on the aircraft as crew and as such was given the clear to proceed.

I was indeed, briefed up on the mission and each helicopter was to carry a USL and then once released move forward and down onto the ground inside Sangin DC to clear the cargo (barbed wire, ammunition always and some food and water) and troops.

The USL was a single net to the centre hook. The Chinook can take up to three individual loads, one on each hook or a tandem load like the ISO. This was a basic resupply (Resup) of everyday items. There was one walking wounded and a few troops to bring back, nothing out of the ordinary.

What was out of the ordinary was the fact we had to go to such lengths to get in there because of the enemy.

At 22:30, the Chinooks were started up but a fog had descended over the area and we had to postpone the start until about 01:00.

The fog cleared and we again started up, collected our cargo and troops and moved to the USL park to pick up the single point netted load. With everything in or attached, the three chinooks lifted and we climbed to high level for the initial transit. We didn't have an Apache escort this time, instead, we would have ground artillery to aid in our landing at the DC.

A few minutes out from the Sangin DC, we descended into low level, when I say low level we were between 40-50 feet of the deck with a USL attached. Usually, you would give a two minutes call on the radio and signal to the troops in the cab, two minutes.

At that time, two minutes out, a battery of 105s (they are called the L118 Field Gun but we call them 105s as they fire 105 mm calibre shells) artillery guns opened fire and started shelling specific targets around the DC complex and town area. They were targeting known firing positions that look down on Sangin DC or the paths in and out.

The town had been deserted by the locals long ago due to the fighting. One minute out and we passed by on our right-hand side, a battery of 81 mm mortars that were now, also joining in with salvos of mortars; impressive sight on NVGs.

Over the desert, descending into the ditch, up over the bank and we see the DC and walled compound, we had to raise the height to get the USL over the wall and then we saw the phenomenal light display of 3 heavy machine guns and

167

7 machine guns firing into the town and around the roads to stop anyone setting up either a firing line or an RPG attack.

I can honestly say I flipped my googles up a couple of times to see the hundreds of rounds of tracer going out from the compound, it was effing awesome.

The lines of tracer streaming down the streets and at known firing point locations coming out from the DC. Huge lines of green tracer and red when off goggles sped towards a vanishing point in the distance just like lines drawn by an artist that sees all parallel lines close together.

We flew over the wall, descended, voice marshalled the load onto the ground, released the load and moved forward and down passed the ditch that runs through the landing site halfway and landed on. Ramps down, troops out and then we felt the force of the percussion of the exploding shells falling the other side of the wall onto Wombat wood.

It was impressive as the blast wave would push through the open windows and doors and you would feel it through your body. Kit off and cargo off, troops back on and we were ready to lift in no time.

We all took off and all headed in the same direction as given by the firing teams, one to stop the nasties targeting you and two not to fly into your own shelling and mortar landing sites.

It was a job well done and the local radio traffic from Taliban FM was, they didn't have enough time to get to their positions and it was too hazardous. Nice one army.

We returned to base and after unloading, de-kitting and debrief, the adrenalin ran out and I just fell asleep immediately. I had been up for nearly 23 hours and really, I wouldn't have missed it for anything, it was amazing.

The Face on TV

2007 saw a lot of fighting and casualties in Afghanistan, it was one of the USA's worst years so far for deaths with a toll of 111. That would change in the years to come, with the tally climbing year on year with wounded casualties reaching thousands a year because of IEDs (Improvised Explosive Devices) or booby-trap bombs.

This isn't about the Americans though, this is about one British man who gave the ultimate sacrifice but will always be remembered by me, unfortunately hauntingly so. I was again deployed and again on Casevac duties when a call came in to pick up a severely injured British soldier, he had been shot by a sniper.

We were as always on our way as fast as we could to retrieve the casualty and get them back to Bastion's main hospital ASAP. We would have an Apache escort due to the location of the enemy and that the troops were, as far as we were told, still in the fight.

Having located the area, we descended, landed and disgorged our MERT team. This was Tier one category casualty, it was serious, this soldier needed surgery as soon as we could get him back.

The MERT rushed on with the stretcher, lifting the stretcher to get up the ramp, the blood poured off the back of the stretcher, which had pooled when the stretcher was level. It, to me, was pissing out and I was quite surprised by the amount but came to realise that a lot of head wounds are very bloody.

This poor sod had been shot through the back of the head and it had exited by his left eye, straight through. The MERT went to work and we got airborne. The nature of the injury meant it was more imperative to get this casualty to the hospital than the Apache escort or even the vibration of the aircraft.

The looks and the hectic work rate of the MERT were the biggest indicators to us and as such, we decided to speed ahead and leave the Apache escort behind. This guy needed every opportunity and luck he could squeeze from anywhere.

We approached Bastion and through the comms relay to Ops, we got a message for a full team to meet us at the landing pad. We landed, the ramp came down, the stretcher and casualty were straight onto an ambulance with a full med team waiting and a surgical team ready at Bastion. It didn't hang around and was gone before we could lift the ramp.

For the crew, that was us, complete for that mission besides restocking and cleaning the cab. Our Chinook engineers volunteered to clean up the blood on the cab, they felt more connected to the events and also there was a little monetary extra for work of an objectionable nature.

We reset the equipment, sorting out kit and back to the tent for the next call. We would only complete four days on the Casevac helicopter routine as a crew, as we were on call 24 hours a day and it didn't matter how many calls you received or at what time you received them, you were that vital lifeline.

Why four days, well, if you get a call every few hours because of casualties like anything, you become fatigued. Carrying fatigue over days becomes cumulative and as such your response time, ability to function and ultimately the ability to correctly assess dangers become less focused, to put it bluntly, your bouncing off the walls but with a 20-tonne Helicopter full of passengers.

We always had prayers (bosses chat) at evening time from the Detachment Commander (Det Co) to catch up on the news from the Operational theatre and what was happening, just think of it as conflict area updates. The news could be striking as you would have news on what had been achieved, casualties list and what the troops would be trying to achieve.

You would also be updated on the ongoing activity and potential new missions. This news would also cover other areas and certainly other nationalities and we would hear often of loss of aircraft especially helicopters from the American forces.

This was important as we would have to resupply, understand the lay of the land from a threat situation and whether we were on for a prolonged fight with the Taliban and inevitably casualties. There was also the usual bollocks about such and such visit from somewhere wanting to understand what was going on and somebody complaining about something.

Sometimes, it got very petty in theatre as the inevitable cock waving by ranks, regiments and sometimes services trying to diminish the good work of others. However, usually being one of the first assets assigned to a new conflict, the Chinook is worth its weight in gold (as the Apache also became with providing that extra edge for the troops on the ground; to the point of life changing or correctly life-saving.

Along with first in, go some elite troops and for many a conflict, the Chinooks found themselves working alongside the Paras and the Royal Marines. For us, there is certainly a bond between these forces and we worked very closely in ensuring we could try to deliver everything they asked for.

These troops had an excellent ethos and it was a pleasure to participate alongside these regiments. The British Army had grown substantially from the second Iraq war and their fighting skills were honed and battle-hardened.

I believe that post both Iraq and Afghanistan, the fighting ability of the British was second to none, I just think the resources were formidably short to assist them. I also found that the Para's and Royal Marines seemed to have greater flexibility or freedom of manoeuvre to achieve their tasks than the greater main army.

It was, for me, far more rewarding to task and use your experience and knowledge to help achieve their aims rather than the inflexible, long-handled screwdriver from someone behind a desk 50 miles away. This does come down to asset usage and obtaining the most out of the least, so I do understand the requirement and knowing that I didn't have the 'Big Picture'.

This was a busy few days for Casevacs and we had another few weeks left in Theatre until another flight from the Chinook helicopter colony of RAF Odiham came out to relieve us. A few pages from my 2007 diary say it all.

Diary

22 April: Into Sangin and FOB Rob (Just outside the green zone) several times: No enemy and ground taken.

26 April: We were targeted by small arms. Too far away and not noticed by lead cab (us), picked up by No 2 in formation, no action taken.

Completed leaflet drop of "If you stay you will die" written on them around Kajaki. A ploy to give the enemy the wrong direction.

30 April: Op Silicon starts tonight. Troops into Garesk to the northeast to sweep. Many aircraft and troops. 10 high-value assets, Taliban, in the Valley of Darkness. Massive moves to hit targets and take the fight to the enemy before the end of the poppy harvest.

And so it's started, Digger and his crew (Kluth, Gunny and Pete W) tasked in the morning on Incident Response Team (IRT, or the Casevac aircraft) and then had five shouts. 24 hr working period, the boys are shattered. The latest Landing site (LS) had enemy firing points and a firefight ensued with the ground troops.

1 May: We took over MERT from these guys. Three calls so far. First to the East side of Garesk, family in a tractor-trailer (possibly trying to get out of the fight) blown up by IED (See Tipping Point). We turned up and deployed Force Protection. Sad state as 9 injured, Granny head wound, 3 male with one being T1 chest injury. 1 male teenager, slight head wound and shrapnel in his foot. Then, four young children, 1 x T1 chest wound serious about 2 years old. All children carried not above 3 years old with shrapnel, burns and cuts. Not a good trip.

Second, trip to pick up near Garesk, Tib Fib from mine strike. Stayed on the ground for 10 minutes to reset lower leg as at 90-degree angle (the soldier was in an Armoured Personnel Carrier APC but because of his leg displacement couldn't actually get out of the door until the morphine had taken and the medics could move the leg).

Third trip: Fort Dwyer, chest pains potential cardiac T1.

2 May: Op Silicon still ongoing from the 2 x 9 ship (two waves of nine helicopters) insert a couple of days ago. Future Ops, possible that a British Air Assault will take place to insert elements into the green belt.

2 May: First MERT shout picked up 1 x Tier 3 casualty and the second shout picked up 5 detainees all with injuries. Flight into the green zone 4 x adults, 1 x teenager all with shrapnel and gunshot wounds.

Third trip, pick up 4-year-old boy fallen from a rooftop and been unconscious for an hour.

3 May: 5 am shout for Tier 1 19-year-old British soldier north of Kajaki mine strike. Right foot missing, shrapnel to both legs, groin and both arms.

06:30 for Tier 1, 22-year-old British soldier gunshot wound to the head near Garmisir. Lots of bleeding in a very poor state, not looking good.

Call 3 10:45 to FOB Rob to pick up 5-year-old girl involved in RTA, she will lose her arm as only hanging on with veins and sinew.

8 May: Nellies crew, who for the first time I am not on, as crew has changed around comes under fire. Roughly 10 rounds into the aircraft. Utility hydraulics down, pilots armour worked and the ballistic protection hit along with the tyres.

This was a crazy time and very Adrenalin filled with missions, raids, attacks and recovery along with normal routine tasking (if anything was normal anymore).

Our detachment finished and we handed over to the incoming crews and headed away from Afghanistan from one extreme location to one that was completely alien to us, home.

Back at home, we were having weeks off trying to acclimatise to normality, whatever that meant. I used to see the news and be saddened when there were reports of casualties and deaths continually on TV.

Wooton Bassett became quite an outpost of moral support for the repatriation and showed what felt to us that someone cared when we came home. We couldn't believe what we sometimes heard on the news or the fact that what was going on wasn't on the news.

This was also a gripe that carried on from Iraq that we felt the British troops were not being understood or appreciated. If the real tally of casualties came out at the time, then I feel the British Public would have been rather aghast at the actual numbers, but with anything that has a touch from a government department, it's twisted, re-written, numbers fuddled and played down.

Sitting at home, watching the news at night, a report came up that a soldier had been buried. What came up next was a picture of that soldier and it froze me instantly. What was a soldier on a stretcher on my aircraft, was now a face on TV and it humanised him to me; it was his funeral.

I was in bits and had to go out to the kitchen to shed those tears away from the in-laws and my wife. I don't know what came over me or why, at that moment or that particular soldier, for I had carried plenty of other wounded and unfortunately dead soldiers before.

It really did cut me up, but I wonder, if I had been waiting for an excuse to expunge what had been building up in me over the years. I still recall the name of that soldier and as a point of remembrance have included him on a tattoo on my back.

What did give me some peace was that he died in hospital with his family by his side, that's quite an achievement since he died on the cab on the way to Bastion but was brought back by the MERT fighting for his life on our aircraft. I don't think it's a point of never forgetting, I think for me, it's a point of always remembering.

To me, it feels like the final stages of the film, 'Saving Private Ryan', when he touches the gravestone of the man that gave his life. It's acknowledging, that they will always be remembered and NEVER forgotten for the sacrifice that was made.

There is something that may sound a bit awful or callous but isn't meant to and please don't take it as such.

'Don't feel sorry for the dead, feel sorry for those left behind as they still carry the burden, the dead don't feel anything anymore'.

My Journey Through PTSD
And Onwards

How do you start writing about this journey having lived through it for the last decade or so, where does it begin, unravel and get tackled? You have already read through a bit of what affected me and I've concluded that it was the amount of trauma alongside the ignorance and total disregard of my mental state that eventually took its toll on me.

Several times, I was blunted by tragedy or trauma I witnessed, but I kept locking it all away thinking that is what people do, surrounded by others all in the same boat, witnessing the same thing.

It was a crazy time of continual operations year after year with no end in sight or even a clear goal of what we were supposed to be achieving big picture wise. When you see infantry depositing their injured mates on the back of the aircraft only for them to return to the fight, you do feel guilty about opening up when so many are in a worse place than you are.

While my trigger and actions are unique to me, I believe there are hundreds, if not thousands, of people that could recognise the path of PTSD as their own.

One of the biggest factors with me is history. As a little kid, I would read the Commando comic books, reading about the daring operations and countless heroic adventures. Most films on TV were of the Second World War and how people rose above suffering to carry out the most courageous of activities.

My family history contains a father that did national Service, a Grandfather that served both in the first and Second World War. An uncle that did the same, but was a Naval Aviator in the first and logistics Major in the Army during the second, a great uncle (Horace Charles Richardson 'Charlie') who at 14, served in the British Army rather than go to jail but ended up in France aged 15 with his army papers saying he was 3 years older, and died in Arras in 1917 aged 19.

I have one of his trench diaries and that leaves nothing to the imagination in the sense of shelling, gassing, and trench warfare.

Extracts from Charlies Diary

At 7 PM—We went into the firing line to strengthen the Manchester Regt. The next morning, one of our fellows was killed by sniping owing to his bobbing up and down.

At about 2 o clock, we were shelled by the Germans, one shell fell right in the trench and blew one chap right out of the trench. Dec 1914-Feb 1915. The next two days were two of hell for we were sitting in water and the only way we could keep ourselves warm was by walking up and down outside on the ground. If the Germans or whoever were in front of us had not been on friendly terms, we would not have been able to do this.

We waited until 11 o clock, but it did not come, oh the agonies of that wait, it broke many a man's spirit. Dawn arrived at last, with us all wet through and to make matters worse for myself, I succeeded in finding the depths of two shell holes full of water by falling in them.

Jan 10—Into the firing line once again, there I had a very narrow escape. Six of us were warned for a guard by an old cart. At about 10 o clock, however, we very soon found we had made a big mistake for the German artillery observer must have seen the cart and taken it for an ammunition limber, for almost the first shell of the day, fell right in the dugout burying two of us, but they got out and we went helter-skelter across the fields back to the company once more.

Mar 4—I had just come back from drawing meat when we heard the peculiar whizzing noise of a shell coming. Of course one and all began to run and a good job we did for the shell pitched in a house about 5 doors from our billets.

Mar 1915—We took over A Coy trenches on the 28 and we had rather an exciting time while there. Firstly, we had two trench mortars flung up at us by the enemy who were no further than fifty yards away from us. The next day, our artillery tried to shell their position but failed horribly, the only damage they did was to wound one of our own fellows.

Here, it was something after the style of the olden time battlefield, for in front of us were a score or so of dead Germans who had evidently been killed when they were repulsed after making an attack a week or so previous.

People talk about the Mound of Death at St Eloi, but this was like being in hell without water. A good name would have been slaughterhouse, but our troops gave it the name Murder Hill.

We did two days in those trenches, quite enough too, and were relieved by the Cameroon Highlanders who had been unlucky with the German trench mortars, one falling in the trench and causing the loss of a section.

We went back in once again and were bombarded for 6 hours, shells of every description were falling thick and heavy, shrapnel, plug shell, whizbangs, stinky pots were hurled at us, but our men kept their heads and marvellous to state only two were injured.

The same night the Germans used gases on the Dorsets and several hundred suffered over it.

On the morning of the 17 Sept, at about 1 o clock, while I was on LP, a German sniper fired at me and luckily the bullet, an explosive one, hit the barbed wire and several pieces struck me in the face. It was nothing serious and I was not over-detained in hospital.

Charlie's Battalion was held in reserves for the early stages of the Somme battle on 1ˢ July 1916 but attacked on the 25th where the battalion lost 450 casualties.

The Devonshire Regt attacked an extremely well defended area near La Coulotte, the Regt history calls this place "a veritable fortress".

It was a hopeless enterprise. Dispassionately, the Regt history records,

"The Devons made a fine effort," they failed to take their objective and suffered 245 casualties, including 70 killed or missing, Charlie was included in the later.

Horace Charles Richardson Killed in Action (KIA), 23 July 1917.

My Great Grandfather served in the First World War and was medically discharged in 1917 because of being gassed. He survived only to work on heavy rescue in the London bombings during the Second World War, staying with a woman for three days that couldn't be saved in the rubble only to catch pneumonia and die himself a bit later.

There are another eight family members who all served in WW1 with Walter William Cox serving in the Royal Navy and also dying due to the war. I was also introduced to The Somme, Ypres, Passchendaele and many other sites in my early teens.

I was left under no illusion of the horror and suffering of war, especially, when both my auntie and parents told me of streets filled with amputees and the blind from the wars selling matches and cigarettes on the street corners when they were kids.

Being woken up on D Day as the noise of so many aircraft getting airborne at 4-5 am. Dog fights high in the sky during bright sunny days and being told to,

"Go home, you silly girl," as my auntie watched the swirls and trails of fighters trying to outmanoeuvre their opponent.

My grandfather never mentioned the First World War, never talked about it but loved the second when he was part of the 52nd Lowland Division and specialised in Mountain and Arctic Warfare.

He, on Remembrance or when listening to the last post played, would turn his back on his kids and walk down to the pear tree at the bottom of his garden to sob. He would also shout out at night and fight in his sleep talking about a head in a barn.

My aunty, at 91, after mentioning that our son went to Wales for an educational week with school, mentioned that they had four weeks in the country picking the thistles out of the carrot field with their bare hands,

"Well, it kept us away from the bombs," she said.

It comes as no surprise that this piss wet through 9 ½ stone weakling at 19 held others in awe at their bravery. Reading and understanding people's courage puts it in perspective a lot of the time. Joining the RAF at 19, I then turned into a 13 ½ stone solid lump in two years.

While I travelled, for the first ten years, exercises were the only thing that really came anywhere close to military action and they were pretty non-descriptive as proper fighting goes. That all changed really for me when I was accepted onto the Airman Aircrew Initial Training Course at RAF College Cranwell.

What started as a three-month initial course lasted for two years and ten months until I became Combat Ready on Chinook helicopters. There, my world and realisation of events that could trigger our mobilisation at a drop of a hat came to the fore.

We were always up for it so to speak, any chance of grabbing your go-kit and hopping onto a Chinook to go anywhere there was trouble or requiring some sort of rescue, we were there.

Many times, the call outs took us to different countries and we would find ourselves completing a NEO or Non-Combatant Evacuation Operation to assist ours and other nationalities escape from certain dangerous areas.

27 Sqn completed a superb detachment helping villages in Pakistan after a devastating earthquake. We were also called out to work in the UK, we helped with a lot of disaster relief with flooding or moving food for wintered cattle or even moving cattle.

Picking up crashed items from vehicles to aeroplanes, most of this came under the title 'Aid to the Civil Power' and while we were happy to help, it all comes down to who will foot the bill.

Above all, we were taught to overcome and find solutions for problems, survive in difficult environments, even evade capture from the enemy on its own territory. We, as aircrew, are classified as High-Value Assets and had to compete the Resistance to Interrogation course.

We all loved that one, not, with the running around being chased by a hunter force, the eventual capture, 18 hours of interrogation in 24 hours, stress positions, white noise and other unfriendly activities to ensure we made mistakes for the staff to manipulate and use. However, the course is there to teach and so it's contents will stay a secret.

I also can't equate to those people who I have picked up in the back of the cab, either taking to or picking up from a fight, not knowing what they went through or what they saw.

While I was trained to do what I needed to do in the back of the Chinook, I don't think I could have done what those men and women did and still do. I find myself immensely proud of their achievements if they walked that ground the enemy held.

So you see, it's not easy caving into something you are unsure of or believe if you did it would impact the rest of the flight in some way. What if you did go sick and someone took your place only to get injured instead of you. It is hard to accept, as at first, you can deal with the issues, they aren't that big at the start or perceived to be.

Over time, the rot starts to decay you from the inside, mentally and then physically but you still carry it with you as it becomes the norm. Looking back, it must have been obvious to others with the way I displayed myself but unless I ask them I'll never know.

I remember struggling when home from deployments and it would take weeks to adjust but it would also take weeks for the family to adjust to me. Reintegrating with my boy and trying to get that level playing field, back into focus again.

My wife Nicky told me it was worse leading up to deployment as about two to three weeks before I left, my total mood would change to focus on the detachment rather than say goodbye to my family.

It was as if I had already crossed the threshold and had cut that responsibility out of my life allowing me to concentrate on what was next. It wasn't nasty just factual and responsive, a bit like an automaton. I think every time I came home, I was a little more broken than then I went out but I never knew what to do as the fog would descend in my head.

Nicky told me that Charlie had asked her about me when she was on the school run one morning. He was about four at the time and the news was on the radio. He heard a report about fighting with the Taliban and Afghanistan and he asked his mum, "Will Dad be killed by the Taliban?"

What could Nicky do except tell the truth? There are some that want to hear that everything is alright and we are all safe, it's not the nature of the job and nobody can really provide that reassurance.

I was asked by my Mother-in-Law how safe would a friend of their family be, being deployed to Afghanistan. What am I supposed to say, he's going to be OK, as much chance as anybody else, what? They wanted reassurances for the soldiers' parents. I couldn't do it, I said:

"If they remain inside the wire at Bastion, then it's the safest place about." I couldn't give the assurance for anything else. I went on to say, "If he goes out in a vehicle then the highest threat was an IED." I was realistic but I hated talking about it. Unfortunately, that soldier got caught up in an IED and sadly died in Afghanistan.

Other people, while very considerate in asking how you are on return, really don't want to know the truth and shied away from the facts. I had returned from a gruelling detachment in Afghanistan and was drinking in the local pub at the time on a Saturday night. A couple came up to me and asked how I was and was everything ok.

I was still in the throes of the detachment cycle really and hadn't de-climatised from the experience. I blurted out, "It was awful, all those fucking kids," I hadn't realised that they had just turned away and left, they must have seen the pained expression on my face and couldn't deal with it. Best not scare the natives and so, I didn't talk about it much after that.

Returning to work in the UK allowed for a fresh start and so, a new focus but it was never long before the flight talked about training up again to return. At the end of my time on helicopters, there wasn't any decent flying to be had in the UK and all flying hours went to the next roulement of aircrew due out.

Year in year out, we barely flew enough hours in the UK to keep us current and many of us didn't stay current or anywhere near that. Too many airframes and hours were needed on operations that it really took its toll on the engineering side and the penalties of such hard graft on the airframes.

There were times when eight crews turned up in the afternoon to fly a two aircraft line at night, each helicopter flying four sorties. We were informed by the engineers that there would be only one aircraft ever that night but we had to plan because of statistics.

When it got to the engineering brief on the main night brief, it would all end up in a bun fight of who needed the hours most and half if not more of the crews went home. It became disheartening to have literally no aircraft available ever.

You can't blame the engineers for this; they, as always, worked like Trojans to achieve the best they could, this was down to money, politics, overusing an asset so its engineering life cycle came around quicker and quicker and this caused huge backlogs. It inevitably played on the psyche that the only hours you were going to get all year were combat hours.

I found myself in a bit of a quandary over time with initially complete immersion in the job that started to fade over the years. I couldn't wait to get onto operations and start flying and getting stuck in.

Within a few weeks, I couldn't wait to get back but as soon as I was, I wanted to be in the fight, in the thick of it. I didn't know what I wanted to do and I was struggling between both places. I didn't want to miss anything or not be involved in the fight. I had become too wrapped up in the entire episode.

I had returned home a couple of months when news struck of an RAF aircraft crashing and killing all those on board, 14 people. It could have been a Hercules but they were not operating in that area.

The numbers didn't tally with fast air and I assumed it was a Chinook and started getting my kit together. There was a sense that the last guys out would go out again as they would still be in date all currencies. It was as if I had to go. It was the Nimrod that crashed.

Yet at RAF Odiham, I felt like I was beginning to become detached, not just from the guys but also the job. I was losing focus and concentrating was becoming harder. I also felt I started to lose areas of knowledge or not be able to retain said information.

I moved Squadrons and became the Deputy Senior Crewman on one of the flights and with the change of responsibility and new crews, I could re-focus and work with and for them. They were a great bunch of guys and I enjoyed their company but I still left the Chinook force Jan 2009.

The Desk officer in charge of our postings had said, if you're on Chinooks, you're doing 15 years before you can move from them. He didn't even know I was leaving the RAF until three weeks before I left. I had completed 10 years on them and had enough but now, as I look back, I think it was entirely due to mental fatigue and trauma issues.

We had already had a few crew people moved because they were fighting their own battles but it didn't seem they were particularly well dealt with and it appeared to be, let's get them away before everyone else gets infected. There was also a don't talk about it attitude from higher up that it felt dirty for the subject to be approached.

I went outside, I was a civvie and I started work for Transport for London on the underground as a trainee Service Controller. I would eventually, once I completed the course, run one of the lines on the underground, acting as one of the Operations Managers in running that particular line.

I had difficulty fitting in realistically, I was like a square peg in a round hole, seeing a multitude of areas that could be developed but I had not come against a union before. As a part of our training, we were invited to sign some information giving up a monthly allowance to join the union.

The union rep was nowhere to be seen, so we were informed it would be better to sign up. I don't think any of the four military guys on the course did and it got back to the union chiefs and they were not happy.

I met some great guys there and really interesting people that had stories of life that were colourful. I learned all the signallers' duties, learned how to drive the trains and walk the tracks. It was quite interesting but I didn't fit in and left. I saw too many unhappy people and realistically, the workplace felt unhappy.

Others used the system to their advantage at getting one over on management and other personnel, there sometimes seemed to lack integrity. There was also a lack of basic knowledge, with some of us in the military we were trying to teach one person in our lessons the phonetic alphabet only to realise he didn't know the English alphabet and he was a train driver.

It could have been just me pushing more than I should have been and getting wound up at others that didn't raise their game. It wasn't in my job description and who was I to start questioning their system.

With that, I phoned the new desk officer and I joined up again as I was a lost soul and didn't know what to do. Many friends offered me positions in companies that dealt with the military but I felt secure and so went Merlin helicopters. I had screwed my pension up with re-joining as I would have to start again but I was in work and thought I would be happy.

To be honest, I fucking worked hard for the people on Merlin's and there were some absolute legends on there, but that wasn't reciprocated by a few and ultimately I reckon it was the worst posting I had ever had. After the heavy landing in Afghanistan, I couldn't wait to detach myself and clear off to fixed-wing.

I had completed the Fixed Wing Crossover Course at RAF College Cranwell at the end of 2012 and felt a surge of happiness and relief. The course instructors were golden and I loved the people on the course and teaching it, really good lads.

It took until April 2013 when at last it all came to a head. I was on the Tri-Star conversion course and away from helicopters after the heavy landing and had recently stayed in Nairobi after delivering elements of the British Army for their Afghanistan pre-deployment training.

I swam in the hotel pool and was suddenly aware that the pool was less than clean when two locals climbed out still in their underwear. I decided to leave the pool straight away and we returned the next day to the UK.

A few weeks later, I noticed that I was becoming really tired and on a four-mile run, I ran out of energy and had to stagger back to the accommodation after mile two and sleep the rest of the day.

Within a couple of weeks, I had an ear infection that perforated my right eardrum and stopped me flying. With the usual dose of antibiotics, I started to feel better after a few weeks, when suddenly I fell very ill.

What started as a global headache just got worse and lasted five weeks. During this time, I lost the ability to speak more than three words and had a thought process of about five seconds before the bubble burst.

I was in a goldfish bowl of life that reset every few seconds. I would turn a tap on and by the time I had turned around, I had forgotten it was on. And so, it carried on for months, flooding the kitchen, putting hands in hot water, setting fire to food, not eating as I would forget what I went into the kitchen for and sleeping 18-20 hours a day.

Visits to the military doctors were met with, it's your ear, it will get better, I even had to write down what I wanted to ask. Eventually, the headache disappeared and I was left with the after effects, having to relearn words and build sentences, slurring and difficulty in concentration.

Two emails at work took two hours and I was continually sent home as not effective. I had lost both the three-month Fixed Wing Crossover course at Cranwell and the four-month Tri-Star conversion course. I had no memory or short-term memory.

After about four months, I realised that I didn't recognise myself or my voice and would mouth words in the mirror to see if it came back. I was still at home the majority of the time and by September, things had started to get worse in work and with the family.

I had a vicious temper and would verbally lash out at everything and anything, a few times it got close to punch ups with people in the streets and I realised it was getting bad when I was driving my car but facing backwards giving a farmer a hard time.

In my mind, he was out of order, maybe he was, but the response was way over the crime, so to speak. I wanted to hurt him really badly and he was a massive guy with shovels for hands but in my mind's eye, he was going to get hurt, badly.

At home, I would chastise my lad for the smallest misdemeanour and be aggressive and shouty (I still hold such shame for my actions and even though my lad is growing up to be a marvellous young man and we are so connected and close, I can't find any forgiveness in my actions).

There was a time that Nicky would dread coming home from work, not knowing what mood I would be in or even if I would be alive.

She said later it was like treading on eggshells, you didn't know when the next explosion would come. There were more than a few occasions when I didn't think I should be here anymore.

It is very strange, thinking about suicide as it doesn't come out like that or it didn't to me. Going through that black period in Aug-Dec 13, dark thoughts would creep up on you in the most unexpected way. You would wonder if it would be better for everyone else if I wasn't here, is this the only life I'm going to know, am I going to get better.

So many thoughts that popped into the head about your demise. For some reason, I believed if my wife had found me, as in my body, she would have hated it but would have understood I couldn't take the pain anymore.

What stopped me was my lad, how would he have coped growing up, what state would I have left him in and how fair was that to him if I had just fucked off and dropped him on his ass for the rest of his life.

I couldn't do it and that's what kept me here, but I did go to see a locum doctor and virtually held him hostage to get some help. I think that was in November 2013 and soon I was started on Citalopram, an antidepressant drug which for me was given for two things, one, to sort out my crazy sleeping patterns and two, stop the madness in my head.

It never sorted my sleeping patterns out but it did stop the fighting in my head and levelled my mood. I was suffering from chronic fatigue now and short-term memory loss, loss of cognitive ability and mental function when I was tired. This continued for several years and continues today but I have learned to deal and work with this fatigue and memory loss.

In one year from Jan 2014, I lost both parents and my twin sister (two of them to Cancer and Dad being a stupid git, banging his head off a radiator), none of which actually affected me or I was emotional about.

I initially put this down to the Citalopram but have realised post counselling that this may not be the case. I, however, was getting more and more emotional about the events in Afghanistan and the fatalities of British troops, I would sob at Remembrance services uncontrollably and in front of everyone.

Every time I talked to someone about an aspect of military life that was traumatic, I would have a lip wobble and shut it out or turn away. I never learned to deal with these and every time I went on detachment, they got bigger and more of them were stored away.

In the New Year of 2014, I wanted to know what was wrong with me as I couldn't figure it out. As far as I was concerned, I had a perforated eardrum which I picked up from Nairobi and the infection went into my head some weeks later and caused all of my problems.

I had been given a Lumbar puncture in December 2013 (7 months post-infection) and it showed raised bands but this was put down to the ear infection and no explanation was offered on what the bands meant.

I saw the Senior Medical officer (SMO) on the station and wanted to know what was wrong, I was told that they didn't know what it was and I had to get used to it and move on.

That didn't help me. Nearly a year had gone by and I was still losing my memory after every few days and continued on trying to complete too much in the effort in clawing my way back to work.

This would cause my chronic fatigue to drop me off that cliff every day in a boom-bust cycle. I would try so much to go to work and used the family weekend time to recoup. I would sleep every afternoon for about 3-4 hours because a couple of hours in the morning had burnt me up.

I never returned to full-time work in the military and at most completed three, two-hour days a week.

In August 2014, I attended the Chronic Fatigue Course at Headley Court and saw others in situations like mine. It was a great group and like Headley Court, full of very experienced and nice staff.

I learned about pacing and trying to come up with decisive plans to help me. These were great but as with my memory, unless put into place every day, within a few weeks, most things just disappear.

Two years after my initial headache, I was seen by the medical board at RAF Henlow. This was to decide whether I was fit enough to remain in the service. What was mentioned by the pre-board doctor isn't what happened on my notes after the board saw me.

I was told there wasn't a primary diagnosis by the Flt Lt doctor but as a secondary on Chronic Fatigue and TINU syndrome (an autoimmune disease that cleared up with drugs).

I was to be 'robustly medically discharged' on the highest possible category never to darken their doorsteps again. When my medical board documents arrived from them, it showed my primary diagnosis as the Chronic Fatigue and TINU.

I also received my pension letter from the UK Veterans agency and was disgusted that I didn't receive a pension. I honestly thought I had caught something from the swimming pool but since the investigation was so long in coming, I will never know.

The pension letter said while I couldn't work at my primary job, I could get "gainful employment" full time, the day after I left the services. How does that work? I haven't worked full time for the last two years and I have Chronic Fatigue that floors me after a few hours awake.

I had been given the highest medical category for discharge but that provided nothing towards my pension. There is, I believe, a disconnect between the medical board and the pension people.

When I called the pension people about my lack of pension, I was informed they didn't use the medical board documents I received, in that case, what information do they use to substantiate a medical pension?

There was only one thing to do and that was to fight the system and appeal. It's still ongoing to this day and after nearly 7 years, they are still asking for information. It fucking galls me to think I now have a proper diagnosis yet they are still splitting hairs at every turn.

There are thousands of veterans that have served that should be receiving a pension yet the red tape is extraordinarily difficult and the system is designed to reduce the chance of payments rather than look-after serving and veterans personnel.

It is extraordinary the amount of money that is wasted on arse projects that don't get off the ground yet the very people the government sends to sort out their failings are left to rot and fester.

Look at the forces now, smaller than at any time in history and less effective, couldn't go to war properly and most, can't even recruit to fill their gaps.

I appealed to the medical board and their reply was, they can only go on what the two pages of information they are given by the medical centre. I appealed to the medical centre that I hadn't been diagnosed correctly and certainly not mentioned anything about my memory, functioning state and mental stability or instability.

I found doors shutting quicker than I could open them and delays by months for notes from the board, it took me several months to obtain my medical notes from the medical centre and then not fully complete.

It all pushed me towards my exit date so I couldn't complain about facts if I didn't have them to hand. I left on Christmas Day 2015, 28 years and 11 days service. Once I was out of the door, nobody wanted to know and then I received my full medical documents from the Station Medical Centre.

I put in a Service Complaint, what should be a 28-day process by their own rules, took 3 ½ years, that takes some beating. The continual writing to officer Commanding P1 which deals with these complaints served no purpose and I heard nothing of any change for over a year.

I complained directly to the Station Commander and we eventually started the process all over again as it had been stalled somewhere in the system. The reply from the doctor was from the same doctor whose reports I was questioning in the Service Complaint. It seemed rather odd to have the same person to review his own work. Talk about an incestual investigation.

The delaying tactics from the medical branch stopped me from arguing my point until it was too late and I was now a civilian. They also pointed out that service complaints cannot be carried out on the medical branch and so the information I was asking for didn't materialise.

The only way to get answers is to go down the legal route but since I had just lost £54K a year and my job and we had to sell the house and move because we couldn't afford the mortgage, we didn't have the money for this either.

I did receive a lot of help during the Service Complaint process from a good friend and neighbour that had far more capacity, energy and intelligence than me. I was, however, informed by the RAF, I couldn't have any of his help or any others except what the RAF would provide for the service Complaint.

So, they were saying this man who knew me and had all my lengthy details and could help me with my complaint wasn't allowed to be used because the RAF didn't want him to.

They did offer a person from the RAF who could help me, which I thought a bit useless as they didn't know me or what had happened and were at least two hours away from where I now lived. You couldn't make it up really like a spoilt child with all the cards.

Life was kind of normalising and I had completed a Chronic Fatigue Course run by Bath Rheumatoid Diseases held in Salisbury in November/December 2016. I was continuing my medicines to control my outburst and mood swings and I still had the continual boom/bust cycles and slept a lot of the time.

What it did was reorganise my priorities and I understood I had been looking in the wrong direction for so long. Instead of being the person that would always put his hand up and help, trying not to be the one with the problem, I stopped that.

I looked inward towards my family instead of outwards and rather than spend what little battery I had for other people and using my family time as the recharging time, I used it for them. For four months leading up to May 2017, I think we as a family, started to become one again.

Nicky had stood by me for four years; she was about to stand by me again. I think coming to terms with what I had been left with and deciding to crack on come what may, allowed time for my brain to start trawling through the unprocessed elements left behind.

We were at the Malvern show in May 2017 and I had been feeling unwell for a couple of weeks going to the doctor saying that I felt something like popping candy going off in my brain.

I would get breathless, finding it hard to feel I was getting oxygen even with a deep breath. He reassured me that it was ok and if I was feeling better, then it should pass.

I felt that unwell that I sat on the grass and then lost the ability to speak and move. The ambulance was called and apparently, I started fitting. The ambulance stopped twice on route to bring me back from going unconscious.

I was told, not that I remember much, that I spent three days in intensive care fitting until they subsided. I went onto the ward and started to come round. I was now back to where I was four years previously, couldn't walk more than a few minutes this time but speaking was ok and very tired.

The hospital completed loads of tests including for epilepsy but all were clear. I returned home but not with any Citalopram and the black cloud enveloped me again for months. It was a horrible time in the house and all down to me but as always, without the medication, I cannot control myself.

This has been like this since 2013 and is still the same today but for the constant medication. That cloud became very dark and again the thoughts of not staying like this appeared to me many times and also was apparent to Nicky, by not knowing what she would find on coming home from work. She couldn't live like this, nor could our boy and nor could I.

I had three episodes of coming off Citalopram up to that time but every time I had reverted to the madness. It crept up over a few days as the Citalopram wore off. I would find myself talking in my head, starting to bite at people and be a bit quick, small things grew to be mountainous arguments.

I started to get paranoid and would have verbal fights in my head with hypothetical arguments that would inevitably turn to fighting. The thing is, I believed I was right and the argument was just. It turned very ugly, very quickly and what manifested itself as anger in my head turned to rage outside.

I would look for trouble, I wanted to argue and I wanted to fight. It got to the point that I could see someone coming down the street and by the time they got to me, I had figured out an excuse to have a go and wanted them to act as the trigger.

It was always going to head into violence and I didn't care, I wanted the fight, I wanted the odds to be so dramatically bad that I died fighting, I wanted the noble cause to hurt and maim as many as I could.

My dreams or nightmares would manifest themselves into attacks and raids and defences, I would lash out in my sleep and found myself fighting the bedside cabinet. In my head whilst trying to sleep, images would flash into my brain just quick enough that I thought I knew it but it was too quick to see and another one would come. And another, and another until it was like a shutter of a film but each frame was a different picture, it went so fast and it never stopped.

It got to the point when I didn't know if I was dreaming or awake and what was going on was real or not, that was frightening. My dreams were becoming my reality and vice versa, that horrible feeling when you think you have woken up from a dream but you haven't and are still in it, then you do wake up and it's with you still, stretching the very fabric of your reality. I had a few days that I didn't know if it was real or not.

I was asked to see a Consultant Neurologist in Salisbury called Dr Ghosh. We talked through my history from my time in the RAF and the headache and what had happened since. He took me into his consultancy room and asked me about two specific things I had talked about.

It was here that it all came out, sobbing for minutes and minutes. I couldn't turn it off and realised that I had come to the end of that particular journey. We saw him a few times and it was a realisation that I did indeed need some help.

It still took me nearly a year to believe him that I had PTSD and it wasn't some kind of organic infection from the ear that entered my head. The fitting in 2017 had been dissociative seizures from the PTSD; physical manifestation of the mental challenge.

Through Dr Ghosh, I was given a contact for a group called Veterans Mental Health Complex Treatment Service (VMHCTS), it is these people that have done what no one else has, and given me my life back. It isn't where it was and it will never be there again, but let's continue with the journey.

The seizures were explained as shell shock in old fashioned terms, I had got to the point where my brain was not going to accept any more input and not being able to control what was going in with the leaking traumas sent me over the edge. They were dissociative episodes where the brain detaches itself from normal functioning to protect you.

I went to see the team at VMHCTS and throughout 2018 was assessed and made ready for counselling. A diagnosis of Complex PTSD was made and so the start of a new journey began.

I had accepted that this was the cause and I had accepted the help that was on offer. The multitude of visits I had to complete to prepare me for counselling was remarkable but looking back I see that they had to ensure I was safe enough and ready to start the process.

The fact that I was ready to face my demons was the biggest hurdle as I didn't know what to expect. It was time to face reality and learn what was going on.

Therapy

Like most of this book, I'm going to be blunt and straight to the point. It's not going to be easy or an easy read for some. For others, it may cause them to remember traumatic thoughts but I hope it encourages the brave to have that extra courage to come forward and tell their story.

For far too long, the mimicry of trauma in social media has downplayed the real requirement in who need help. Having PTSD for being called a bad name isn't PTSD.

With my counsellor, a Dr Gemma Parry, we started quite softly on understanding what it was I wanted out of these therapy sessions. It took time to accept my counsellor, as anything, it's where do you fit in, how does this thing work and what should I do?

What was the aim for them, as if you cannot identify what you wanted then how do you know you have got there? Your aims can change as the sessions expand your understanding but for the beginning, it was the little girl in the white dress and the soldier who was shot through the eye.

Later on, it would materialise that these were not the only issues and not the only reasons for my traumas. I wanted to be able to talk about events that had happened without getting upset, to do that, you have to confront them. I also wanted to be able to see military events on TV or at Remembrance without turning on the waterworks or having a lip wobble.

The main focus is with the therapy itself and that can take many different forms. I was offered EMDR Eye Movement Desensitisation and Reprocessing and the old-fashioned talk therapy.

I chose to talk with a little Cognitive Behavioural Therapy (CBT). I couldn't complete the EMDR as they may trigger seizures and having had a few and losing my driving licence for some time, I didn't want to return to walking with a stick and sleeping 20 hours a day.

It took quite a few sessions before we got to the point where I talked about one of the events. There was a definite build-up towards the initiation of this and I instigated it on the day, saying I was ready to face one of my demons.

The VMTCTS worked through a three-way route of which the initial is stabilisation. This format builds you up to the point where you can start the therapy process. The staff have to be sure that you are fit physically but more essentially mentally fit to be able to cope with their therapy strategies.

This can take months and months but they want to ensure that returning to some of those traumas and processing them is not going to send you into a downward spiral. You will visit places that you have stopped yourself from doing so many, many times, and it is upsetting and unsettling, they know what they're doing, do you?

Once the staff are content that you fit the criteria, you can start the therapy. This is the meat on the bones of the sessions and analyses so many areas around the traumas, it's very educational.

Lastly, it is the re-integration to allow you to carry on with your life and understand what path you want and can take, how to continue to deal with the issues that concern you and how to cope daily if they resurface.

The following chapters are taken from my notes that Dr Gemma Parry and the team took throughout the year and a half they spent with me. Some are written as they wrote the notes, others are me telling what I did and how I saw it.

Stabilisation

The stabilisation will cover the following areas: Knowledge of PTSD Psychoeducation module, sleep module, emotion regulation and management module, physical health and fitness module.

What they identified: My frustration and anger at a continual ongoing Service Complaint.

What they gave me to help me during the process: Sleep hygiene, cutting out caffeine, reducing alcohol. Breathing exercises to adjust the mind and reset it, a safe place in my head I could escape to that would calm me down and other relaxation techniques.

Struggling to sleep for over six years: I would have meticulous planning of very philanthropic ideas, always planned, very detailed and driven.

Struggling to manage expectations, needs to train. Continuing struggle with cognitive functioning and memory loss.

Dark thoughts and unwanted images (these would increase as the therapy started), dreams took on a more violent texture, shot by 17-year-old with a shotgun. Arrival at old building with a huge hall filled with striped-pyjama-wearing PTSD sufferers as in the first world war. Patients either quiet, rocking or screaming but the ward was full.

Tearful due to PTSD problems.

Struggling to relax, could never sit down for long periods. The requirement to sleep in the afternoon due to his CFS.

Find that the largest activity used in the brain is drive and only relaxes when taken out of the environment that he has no control. He controls threat systems by staying in his comfort zone.

Understanding that putting too much into an agenda and never achieving the small goals. Must learn to reduce or be realistic.

Introduce coping and grounding strategies. And appreciate the better times and feel their worth but understands the elation is capped. This also stops him descending below 4 on a scale and coming under the influence of the 'Black Dog' dark cloud and dreams of fighting to the finish, hand to hand and battling unbelievable odds in defence of some righteous endeavour.

It also stops the explosion of anger and paranoia build-up looking for threats and having an excuse for a fight. It also stops the suicidal thoughts from emerging.

Identified that medication stopped him expressing his emotion and to a lesser intensity. Trauma Therapy may help him in releasing this. Discussed that trauma therapy will increase his emotional intensity and has to understand that it could lead to more disturbing items entering his head.

The last two sessions, we covered from his childhood up to the present day and work throughout this.

The patient asked if myself and he could develop a less clinical approach to the sessions as it felt too medical professional and patient based and he needed a companion who he could feel comfortable to offload to.

I watched a program on TV about an Ex-Special Forces guy called Jason Fox 'Foxy' talking about PTSD called 'The Final Mission: Foxy's War'. I couldn't believe it, there was I, alone at night watching this guy talk about all the things he went through with PTSD.

There was me in my living room jumping up and down going,

'And me, that too,' when I discovered I had the same shared experiences with my PTSD. It was an illuminating experience and one of which I couldn't wait to tell my wife the next day.

I asked both my wife and son how I came across to them, I didn't expect to hear their answers and the responses definitely grounded me in a realisation of what they see. That was my last stabilisation session and had taken six months to achieve the desired level for me to start therapy.

Other Adventures

National Standby is a 24 hr—365 day a year call out for many a group of military personnel. For the Chinook Force, it means being airborne anytime day or night within two hours of receiving the call. One such call was to pick up the Prime Minister at the time, Tony Blair.

It was 7 July 2007 and the London Bombings had just happened. We were tasked to pick up the PM from RAF Northolt (he was away with the EU Summit in Scotland) and fly him into central London.

A strange day as London has very restricted airspace with Gatwick and Heathrow to the south and west and very strict rules about flying over the capital city. We were cleared by air traffic after a code-worded call sign and we were asked if we wanted all Heathrow traffic to be diverted for us to travel through their airspace, we went around.

There was only one other piece of traffic over London and that was the air ambulance. We picked up Tony Blair and he sat right next to the open front door, no helmet, no ear protection. For me, it seemed the noise of the aircraft was so loud that it stopped others talking to him and actually allowed him to think.

He didn't move the entire journey, just watching the landscape of London as we flew in from the west. We landed, I believe, at Wellington Barracks but the Prime minister just sat at the door, nobody went near him and he just seemed very occupied by the event.

When you think about it, his very next actions and words were going to be monitored by the entire world.

Falklands Islands

Some of the most interesting trips tended to be underslung loads and the variety of what could be carried underneath the helicopter on hooks. From Armoured Personnel Carriers, tractors and fire engines to aircraft and helicopters to 105 field guns and ammunition, all have been swung underneath.

One of the most challenging USLs was the single point (one strop from the centre hook) ISO container from a ship and then carried to a mountain top in the Falklands Island. There were a few sites that needed resupplies by this means, as there were no roads up to these stations.

Taking the container off the deck of the ship meant breaking the 10ft minimum safety clearance around the helicopter because the ship's crane was in the way. The No2 crewman at the front right hand door used to put his hand on the crane and voice Marshall the lift from the front door.

So there, was a 13-14 tonne helicopter in the hover over the deck of a ship in a swell, so close to a crane, you can touch it from the front crewmen's door, picking up an 8 tonne ISO on a single point to take up a very windy hillside. It used to spin and sway like a bastard but it was the most effective way to get it up there.

There was a considerable amount of ISO traffic up and down from Onion Range, a live-fire range a short distance from Mount Pleasant Airfield (MPA). One trip caused quite a stir when the returning ammunition stored in an ISO container was dropped off at the bomb dump.

I wasn't on the crew at the time but was with the team in the Falklands. There was nothing odd about moving ammunition and placing everything in an ISO container for use, it allowed for a one trip drop off keeping the ammunition dry.

The crew grounded the ISO at the bomb dump and returned to RAF Mount Pleasant Airfield, it wasn't long before the tannoy went out with a huge cordon zone with immediate effect around the bomb dump.

What the armourers had found in the ISO besides lots of unused ammunition was a misfired mortar round with the safety pin missing from the fuse. What was really bad news, is that it was rolling around the ISO as it was flown to the bomb dump along with another 85 loose mortar rounds and 20 detonators.

Nothing had been secured for the return flight to the bomb dump. That little beauty, if it went off would have sent the ISO, Chinook and crew back to Onion range very quickly and in very small bits. There was a board of inquiry within a few days held in the Falklands, I never heard the outcome.

Some rather either ingenious or crazy bastards decided that the run down from one of the hilltop repo sites to the shore area, was far too long to spend in a vehicle and far too dangerous. The tasking sheet for a few days would require the Chinook to carry an ISO from the hilltop site to the beach in the morning and return it the same evening.

This went on for a few days, I am led to believe. The crew thought that it was getting filled up with kit and returned that evening. Something didn't add up and the crew, as per the tasking sheet, picked up the ISO container that morning and took it down to the beach and flew off.

What they did next was dip behind a hillside for the noise of the aircraft to get quieter. After a couple of minutes, they popped back over the ridge to find some Gurkha soldiers letting themselves out of the ISO.

Rather than drive the route twice a day, these lads had decided to hitch a lift inside the ISO container there and back so only requiring a few minutes transit. They didn't get a lift back that evening or ever again.

The Chinook is often multitasked by different agencies and one of the oddest roles is that of an airborne fire engine. We were on our way back to Mount Pleasant after completing our days' tasking but were interrupted for a new task. There was a fire on Sea-lion island and it was slowly drifting across the entire space.

Unfortunately, it hadn't been long since the Sea-lions had given birth and were still nurturing their young. Like much of the Falklands Islands, it is made up of peat and during the dry seasons can catch fire from lightning strikes.

While these don't tend to burn like forest fires raging across the countryside, they still burn through the entire scrub and can go underground.

We attached a device called a rainmaker which essentially is a massive bucket that sits underneath the helicopter and holds water. When you are in the right position, you press a button and open the doors allowing for the water to drop on the point of the fire you want.

We tackled the blaze as best we could, as dropping the water from too high allowed the water to be blown away by the high winds. Dropping it too low caused the rotor blade downwash to spread the flames.

To be honest, it was a bit of a bastard, as we could see the flames engulf the Sea lions that couldn't get out of the path of the flames. We did what we could but it wasn't enough and the entire Island burnt through.

We found out what caused the fire though, a tall ship was anchored nearby but had left the area towards Port Stanley. Some of the ship's crew had decided to go ashore and have a BBQ, even though BBQs were banned on the islands for obvious reasons.

What they did next was to bury the contents of the BBQ which caused the ignition of the island. We met the said crew in Port Stanley a few days later and they left the eatery once they found out who we were and we found out who they were. I think the local government asked them to come ashore for a chat, I hope they got what they deserved.

Again on fire-fighting duties, we were tasked to take the Port Stanley Fire Brigade and generators and at least a mile of hose to West Falkland to stop a fire consuming a farmhouse. At first, we struggled to even identify where the house was and only knew when the family came out and waved at us.

I expected to see flames and smoke but couldn't really distinguish where the fire was. We shut down and the firemen got to work carrying the hose a half-mile to the seashore and setting up pumps etc.

This was a peat fire and we saw wisps of smoke coming up from the ground as it started to burn the peat. While the fire may not have engulfed the house, it would have burnt through the peat that formed its foundations and as such caused the collapse of the house when the peat shelf dropped from the burning.

I think the firemen stayed about eight hours to douse the fire and soak the peat to stop its progression.

Underslung Loads

Having a huge lift capability, the Chinook can lift another Chinook with the blades off and defueled. There are many times that the requirement has been called on, not just from Chinooks but other helicopters also.

Sometimes, it is better to use this lift capability rather than by a road move. This could be because of the location of the item, the road issues and even the threat. Quite a few moves are for aircraft on ranges to be relocated.

I lifted a Puma helicopter in Northern Ireland and we, as a crew, wanted to land the Puma underslung in the landing circle better than the Puma crew would have done if it was flying. We managed it and to get very high scorecards off the engineers on the return for doing just that.

While I was on an exercise in Scotland as a new crewman, I was offered the chance to fly on the aircraft on a weekend job. A light aircraft had crashed in the Forth after take-off and had buried itself into the mud.

While I wasn't operating, I did get the chance to witness the process of lifting the tail and trying to lift the body of the aircraft that had snapped from the tail. The tail came up no problem but the aircraft body refused to move.

Even though only being 7 tonnes, the Venturi effect caused the engines to be sucked deeper in the mud. Eventually, they had to obtain a 30-tonne lifting barge to recover the fuselage.

Qualified Helicopter Tactics Instructor

Having qualified as a QHTI in late 2002, we often found ourselves travelling around the country on exercises or positioning for the next task. Part of the job spec of a QHTI on the Sqn is to teach amongst other things 'fighter affiliation'.

Or to put it into film speak, a dog fight but between a helicopter and a fast jet. Fast jets fall into two categories for this which is agile and radar. An agile fighter has IR capable missiles and most probably cannon, whereas the radar fighter has a radar system to acquire, track and missile guide towards the target as well as IR missile capability and cannons.

The issue with radar equipped fighters (for us on helicopters) is that they don't have to get eyes on to identify you as the target. The Agile fighters have to visually acquire you and identify you as a target due to the short-range nature of the missiles.

This helps us as we have four pairs of eyes looking out for the enemy and a better chance of defeating the fast jet in a fight. There are always tricks up every crew's sleeve, fast or rotary on how to defeat the enemy and not being spotted is the biggest one.

Our Self Defence Suite (SDS) onboard the Chinook can pick up that we are being looked at by another radar (called 'being painted') and can also automatically dispense flares with the threat of an IR missile and we also utilise Chaff with the radar threat. The biggest aid to us would be our intelligence on where and what the enemy had.

One such routine transit in a Chinook saw a single crew heading up North for some work. What he had over the next twenty minutes was the best dog fight ever. We were intercepted by two Tornados GR4s and then by two Harriers.

We, as a crew, controlled the fight from front to back and back to front, honouring the highest threat and passing clock codes on enemy positions and profiles. The Chinook is a versatile beast and can be flown and thrown around the sky, from 60-degree angle of bank on one side to an instantaneous reverse and 60-degree angle of bank on the other.

What we didn't expect is for a Hawk and three American F-15 Strike Eagles to ask to join the fight. It all got rather busy and we were getting bounced from all sides but they were also having a go at each other.

The Harriers departed first and then the Hawk and we had to also continue on our route and left the others battle it out. It was quite extraordinary to watch so many aircraft and all want to fight with us. Good practice all round and the highest tally of aircraft I've had in a fight at once.

While I am sure we would have suffered if this was real, you would be surprised how many times we can defeat a fast jet and get them to disengage rather than continue the fight.

It's not just the manoeuvres and use of chaff and flares, you get a fast jet come too close and a minigun burst at 66 rounds a second, can have a lasting impression on that pilot.

The Goddam Best BBQ I Never Went To

Flying around the UK in 2001 was a bit difficult as we were used to landing on in fields and rough terrain across the country, it wasn't as if the troops were waiting at a bus stop to be collected.

So, when foot and mouth broke out across the country there were a lot of curtailments in exercises and stringent rules to be applied if you did land anywhere other than airfields.

We were greeted at one stop point on shut down having returned from a field landing to a fire engine with firemen wearing HazMat clothing and breathing gear and trays of disinfectant for our boots before we were allowed off the aircraft.

However, once such trip at night took us through the highlands and mountainous region of Scotland. Travelling from east to west around Pitlochry to Oban I think, we were navigating down a valley when I thought I could smell a BBQ.

I was No2 crewman at the front door and the window was up as I was helping to navigate. For some reason, the pilot had taken us up to the northern side as he didn't want to overfly an avoid.

I mentioned to the front that I could smell what seemed like BBQ and then it went and no-one else smelt it. A couple of minutes passed and again the BBQ smell came back, this time the front enders picked it up and then the No1 crewman at the back.

We looked out the windows for signs of a BBQ under our night vision goggles and nothing. Coming up to our turning point at the end of the valley was going to introduce a hard left turn, keeping the high ground to our left.

Our turning point was seen and we updated the pilot the information on the next leg. Turning point approach and a hard left was initiated to a,

"What the fuck is that, climbing," from the handling pilot.

We were going through the blazing funeral pyre of a couple of thousand cattle. We had inadvertently flown straight through the Foot and Mouth burning pyre and our goggles backed down due to the ferocity of the blaze.

As we passed and climbed through the smoke, we could see all the cattle upturned and burning. While that was sad, there was an unbelievable smell of BBQ that was insatiable to quench and clung to your nostrils and clothes for the rest of the journey.

Bosnia Herzegovina

While people still see the horrors of war in the Middle East, Africa and elsewhere around the globe, it wasn't so long ago that Europe was in the middle of a devastating war between a few countries.

Serbia used tensions within Bosnia to start ethnic cleansing of the Bosnian Muslims (Bosniaks) that lived in Bosnia which also saw Croatia brought into the conflict.

It was a ruthless conflict that forgoes the usual conventions of war with systematic genocide committed and widespread killing of men, women and children.

I joined the fray quite late on in the nineties when it was a lot quieter and NATO had taken over the reins from the UN. We were stationed in a Croatian military barracks called Divulje near Split along with several other military nationalities.

We had hardened accommodation and during the summer and late autumn, it was a very pleasant place. We would take off from the helicopter park we shared with the Royal Navy Sea-kings and the Croatian military and out over the water before climbing over the mountains and entering Bosnia Herzegovina, visiting places called Mconic Grad bus depot, Sipovo, Gornji Vakuf, Banja Luka metal factory and Glamoc.

Flying, we used to pass a previously used Winter Olympics ski jump that was mined from top to bottom. A huge freshwater lake that apparently had more human DNA in it than fish life due to the dumping of Tito's old enemies (but that was just hearsay), whether that could change within minutes in the mountains that could trap you in the valley with no IF option to get out and mined land everywhere.

It was an adventurous time but rarely that threatening to us in the helicopters, if anything was going to catch us out, it would be the weather. We picked up all types of military nationalities and placed them all over Bosnia.

If we stopped over somewhere then we went shopping for CDs and DVDs of the latest releases. Having no copyright or piracy laws in force in the country, we would take the opportunity to purchase copy CDs for 1 Deutsch Mark and a DVD for 5 DMs.

On the return journey, the Croat forces used to train on their MANPADs using the SAM 7 shoulder launched missile. As we would approach the Helicopter landing pad, we would see troops pointing the SAMs at us so they would get used to the tones given out by the SAM to indicate when the missile guidance system had locked on to your engine heat signature.

It was a bit surreal at the time but you got used to it. What you didn't do was fly at night when it was New Year's Eve or an important public holiday in Croatia. All the personal automatic weapons and rifles would come out and the collective firing into the sky to celebrate whatever it was, went on for some hours, you didn't want to be airborne for that.

There is a story from another crew that had a very close call with some local inhabitants and the aircrafts minigun. There was a live-fire range we could use inland (which we don't have in the UK for helicopters) called Manjaka Range.

It was used by the Chinook force a few weeks previously and the crewmen got some currency on the gun and a bit of brassing up of old vehicles and buildings etc. This trip was going to be no different and utilising the buildings and vehicles were a good teaching aid for the shooting practice.

As with all ranges, they have to be cleared first and a fly through the area ensures there isn't the equivalent of a Bosnian Sunday dog walker wandering through the patch. The range seemed all clear and the Chinook was setting up its first serial with laying down fire on the houses.

Something had changed according to one of the crewmen and they noticed that some more vehicles had been brought into the range. But rather than scatter them about the range they had been neatly parked outside the house.

This drew some 'what ifs' amongst the crew and just before brassing the vehicles and buildings that uncomfortable gut feeling surfaced in a few of the crew. So they did the sensible thing and halted the firing serial just to make sure the house was unoccupied as it had been weeks previously.

To their surprise, out popped one of the occupants and then more. The whole firing exercise was cancelled and the Chinook returned to base. The news travelled to the range controllers and a team was sent out to investigate.

Would you believe entire families had occupied the houses as they were refugees from the war? They didn't know it was a range but just saw empty accommodation. Now, how much trouble would there have been if the crews had started brassing up those cars and houses?

Croatia is a delightful place to visit and on the whole, we were welcomed but also knew the boundaries of where to and not to go. Curfews were strict and signing in and out of camp a necessity. There was also a booze ban on in any of the blocks but we had a bar in the bottom cellar of a building which served its purpose.

The 'Black Dog' as we called it, had a cage which was used frequently for acts of submission, punishment and general nakedness for all who forfeit the rules of the bar. The Royal Engineers bar had a door to what was supposed to be a set of toilets.

It was in the middle of a wall up about four or five concrete steps. The first time I asked where the bogs were, I was told:

"Up those steps mate."

Off I went and opened the door only to find two things had happened. The first was that I had opened the door to the rest of the brick wall and no toilet.

The second was with the door opened, it pulled a string that ran the length of the roof and rang a bell at the bar which caused me to buy the next round or a crate of beer for the members of the bar, thieving gits but ingenious.

When we did visit Split or Trogir for a night out, it would start with huge beers, food mixed with massive amounts of garlic and finished with the local spirit called Kushkovach which tasted like bananas but was made from pears.

Garlic was definitely in all the dishes. When you ordered something to eat but it didn't say garlic, it would come with it. If you asked for garlic then you would get shavings of the stuff all over.

On our way back from one of our garlic meals we passed a stunning yacht tied up next to the open plaza, it looked costly and new. Picture in your head an 80-100 ft yacht with an open gangplank at the bow of the ship.

If you looked at the stern then you saw a rather large and shiny brass ships bell. We dared one of the crewmen to go onboard and ring the bell and run off. A bit like knock door bunk but this shall be called 'ship bell ring'.

So this guy (Kev H), went on board to do just that. Unbeknown to him, one of the other crewmen snuck up the gangplank and as Kev was about to ring the bell shut the ships gang plank door, banging it up and down, shouting,

"Alarm, alarm, alarm!" at the top of his voice.

We were all in stitches at this moment as Kev's face just dropped and he started to leg it back across the deck to the gangplank. We then noticed the yacht spill out its security with some very large men in very small polo tops running out of the cabins at the stern and following quickly behind Kev in hot pursuit.

We were doubled up laughing at this moment until Kev ran down the gangplank and towards us shouting, "Run" as the security followed him down the gangplank and towards us.

We also started running in the opposite direction but the guards were gaining as we were laughing so hard, we did get away.

I think Bosnia detachment was the only time I nearly got charged. We were attending a function that evening being held I think by the Americans but with some military dignitaries attending. We were warned by the Det Cdr to behave and I was given the task of looking after a bit of a notable crewman for the evening.

He was due to fly in from the UK that day and as such not ready to fly on the Chinooks in theatre until he had completed all the necessary paperwork etc. The Det Cdr told me that this crewman called Andy had to remain sober and not get into trouble. The boss was unusually stern on this occasion and we all wondered what was up with him.

Well, let's just say, it didn't go to plan and this crewman was shit faced. What we did manage was to get him close to the accommodation and so nearly out of harm's way. I was supporting him with my right shoulder and trying to get him further up the road.

Unbeknown to me, my left ankle was right next to a small tree stump and as it turned out this crewman was a lot heavier than I thought so when he fell on me, I went over on my ankle, well I went over, the ankle stayed.

By the time we got back to the room, I am in bits. I take my shoe off and there is a lump the size of a crab apple on my ankle bone. The shit faced crewman then says,

"I've done a battlefield medic course, I'll fucking fix it," and then attempted to get my ankle and straighten it.

"You can fuck off," and I went to bed.

Having to get up early for the day's tasking, I hobbled halfway to the briefing room before realising I couldn't carry out any function. Another crewman took my place and I was then transferred to the local med unit at Sipovo where I spent a few days with the Dutch nurses before returning to the barracks. By the time I returned, the boss was spitting chips and I was sent home to the UK.

Within a week, a Chinook was due to fly out to Split to take over from another airframe and I volunteered to fly on the cab returning to Split. I was still in a lot of pain and once I returned, the boss demanded to see me and we met outside the coffee house on base with most of the rest of the detachment.

While everyone else was pleased to see me, the boss wasn't and made me walk up and down to see if I was fit enough. I tried my hardest to walk normally and pretend I wasn't in pain and that bloody apple had subsided but was still there.

He was convinced and I returned to the flight line and daily tasking. However, I found out later from the other crews that on return from this detachment, the Det Cdr was going to charge me for this misdemeanour.

I think it was going to go down the route of impacting British Forces Capability in theatre. If I hadn't jumped on board and flew the Chinook to Split, then I would have faced a definite career-changing moment.

We always liked a party and we would organise a hangar party at a drop of a hat and push invites out around the station and further afield. There would always be some sort of theme and some of the outfits were extraordinary.

One such party at the Black Dog was held in honour of the release of the movie Gladiator with Russel Crowe. Much cardboard, black masking tape and silver foil were used in the process and shields, swords and armour were made and worn.

We were on our way to the bar marching with togas, weaponry and helmets four abreast when out of no-where a car horn sounded behind us. We shit ourselves and jumped out of our skin with one of the lads (Ginge) taking off.

When we looked around what we saw was the Regimental Sergeant Major (RSM) on his pushbike on the way to the phone booths to phone home. He had placed a car horn on to the handlebars of his bike and was laughing out loud on his way to make a call.

On our way back to the block after our very lubricated evening, thanks to the Czechs who brought some Absinthe, we spotted the RSM's bike. We then saw Ginge nicking said bike and heading back to the block. We nearly got to the door when we heard a bellow from down the road.

The RSM was speed marching up the road and we scattered like rats except for Ginge who was midway trying to place the RSMs bicycle in a tree. We called at Ginge to get a move on with the unrealistic belief that if he got across the threshold of the front door he would be safe.

Ginge made it back and the RSM eventually got his bike back and we waited for the bogus punishment but it never came, a good sport!

The RSM did, however, complete a surprise block inspection which caused minor panic for two of the crewmen (known only as Andy W & Chris S). Not being allowed to buy booze around the camp, these lads had an ingenious idea of ordering delivery pizzas. Not only did they order pizzas, they also ordered large bottles of red wine.

These two crewmen who had two months out in Split had the crazy idea that they could eat enough pizzas that the entire saved pizza boxes would reach the ceiling. So they started on the pizzas and wine and continued to eat and drink throughout the detachment.

When the surprise inspection took place, one of the crewmen whose room it was rushed to the block and saw the RSM outside his door. Thinking on his feet he blurted out,

"Sir, my oppo in the room is sleeping off nights for flying and can't be disturbed."

"Nice try Sergeant," came the reply,

"But I'm on my way out, not in." He continued, "Good effort, but clear it up."

That was it, the RSM had rumbled the boys and the boys knew that and sorted the room out.

Counselling

Therapy

My first therapy session and I was more fatigued than usual, the house becoming a mess and I was not keeping on top of things in my normal fashion. It may have been an unconscious thought of the session to come and my first go at the 'Girl in the White Dress'.

We visited the story and I started giving the account but just started to sob a real deep sobbing that drained the body. I was taken to my safe place by Gemma and left the session feeling calm.

The following week was one of a busy, unstoppable mind which usually meant that I remained active (usually cleaning the house) until I became too tired to carry on and was forced to sleep in the afternoon. This week though, it felt as if parts of my brain had become unlocked.

One of my dreams was of removing a T-shirt to undress only to find another underneath every time. Every time I took one off another would appear before I could get it over my head. So I gripped two-three at a time and it continued on and on leaving me with a feeling of being stuck and not getting anywhere.

I had to detach myself from the dream so the safe place and breathing practices came in and the dream went. The following session, we revisited the traumatic event and I recalled the 'Girl in the White Dress' but it was in more detail but delivered mechanically.

I recall not feeling emotional but detached, an example would be of a dam filling up with water with the dam being my brain and the water my emotional state. Unless or until the dam is full and ready to overflow or spill then I wasn't ready to release my emotions.

The effect of sobbing the previous session had emptied my dam and as such, it would take time before I was ready to be that volatile to do so again (looking back, I shouldn't have to wait for the dam to overfill before it's released but obtain the ability to release anytime I think it needs to flow.)

I realised that I hadn't spoken to my military colleagues since 2012 nor had I wanted to tell them what was going on and what I was doing now.

We discussed avoiding or experiencing emotions is a factor that prevents trauma memories from being processed. And I was very good at being cheeky, a bit funny and changing the topic with Gemma which showed I didn't want or had stalling mechanisms to stop me processing these events. This was the nail on the head moment.

The entire reason why these and other traumatic events had and still trouble me was that I had never processed them as proper thoughts.

Think of it like (yep another analogy) your memory is a linen cupboard and every memory and event is stored there like a piece of linen, washed and folded and put away until used again. When you want the memory, you go to the linen cupboard and retrieve that memory, unfold it, use it and when finished, fold and place it back in the linen cupboard.

With trauma, that memory isn't processed and like the linen cupboard, the sheets are scattered all over the floor. Every time you smell, see, hear, touch something that takes you back to the trauma, it's you tripping up over the linen on the floor.

All that trauma therapy is trying to achieve is that you process the memory allowing you to pick up the piece of linen, fold it up and place it where it should be. That achievement is by far the greatest thing that can happen to your brain, for you at that time.

It defuses the ticking bomb, closes the worry, stops the anxiety and allows you to recover from those episodes that have dominated your life. Will it stop the memories, no, will it stop the crying, no, but it will allow you to accept and continue with a new life.

Be realistic, you've changed and you always will be changed, embrace the fact and get on with your life.

I started to record my therapy sessions where I talked about my traumatic incidents. It is quite weird to hear yourself in those deep, emotional states and I don't even recognise the words or sequence of events as I told them, I am so far detached. I learnt from one of the episodes that I had blocked or lost part of the memory and I cannot recall it at all.

The feeling of worthlessness and incompetence handling the situation came up over and over again. My ability to function was diminished and that sense of guilt and frustration in not being able to deal with the incident did and still does play on my psyche. I think that is why I have never returned to any of the reunions or see old colleagues and mates is due to that feeling.

A good point brought up by Gemma was that,

'This isn't victim Olympics' meaning just because someone else has a worse injury than yourself, it doesn't mean you can't have your issues allowed.

Every single person has had something happen to them, had different training, with different people and are different from each other. You will witness things differently at different times and have different emotions.

The big step is admitting to yourself it is alright to have these emotions. For years, I battened down the hatches, slowly crumbling away like a Norfolk sand cliff face with the onslaught of the weather.

We took a look at my daily life and pattern of events with CFS, my memory and cognitive difficulties. It became apparent that I never returned to anything like my previous self and what I set myself was always bar too high. What I had to do was re-evaluate what is possible and negotiate with myself on realistic terms what I could achieve.

Rather than make a list which I had always done, I changed it to a piece of A4 paper that I split into a 14-day calendar. I looked at the days and using the SMART principle (Sensible, Measured, Achievable, Realistic and Timely) or just the Realistic.

Could I complete what I had written down and being true and realistic with myself, if it was a no then I moved the task to another day? It worked, it unloaded the stress of achieving, I had just learnt how to control a never-ending list of unachievable tasks. It was so refreshing and yet so simple.

I didn't have to justify anything, just move items. This helped to settle things down and if I knew something was coming along that would tire me out, I could plan and include rest days before or after, or break them down into manageable chunks.

In August 2019, it was suggested that I write down my trauma experiences as a way of cataloguing and processing the memories. I started to write but found it difficult to place dates, times and even countries to the episodes as they had jumbled in my brain.

Not only was this going to get things in order for me but I also wanted to write down some funny stories for my son, Charlie, for when he was older. I wanted a record so he would hopefully understand from my point of view what happened.

He is thirteen at this moment in time and yet I still feel it is too raw for him at his age. He will understand the funny stories and we do share the same inane sense of humour. For years, I used my storytelling at bedtime to invent complete out of this world fantasy stories that would include him in the storyline.

Aliens, dinosaurs, him being a helicopter pilot (should have been a crewman), space adventures, rescue missions, that were made up on the spot. His mum used to berate me as when I came back downstairs, you could hear the laughter come from his bedroom.

"And how is he supposed to go to sleep like that?" would greet me downstairs.

Another part of letting go was my continual fight with the MOD for the Armed Forces Compensation Scheme and Pension Scheme. I had challenged them before I left and continue to do so as I had no medical pension. This was grinding me down continually and the effect of having to go through my notes every time to answer the questions was telling.

The 3 ½ years' Service Complaint was a manifestation of a joke that if it happened in the civilian world, would have had their arses screwed quite literally out of the seat of their pants. The continual in our view 'nothing has changed' attitude stank of them finding ways to squirm out of their responsibility rather than fulfil a need that carried over from the military.

I had no way of understanding what I had to achieve to obtain a medical pension or to get where I wanted or how to go about it. There is just no information out there and they give nothing away themselves.

The treatment continued into the end of 2019 and I started getting increased side effects. I started to recall stuff that had been hidden away, my dreams became more vivid and violent with lashing out and shouting in the night.

To me they were very real, the time I was fighting and it ended with me getting stabbed in the face, the being shot by firing squad, every time I fought and fought hard, real knuckle dirty killing.

It came to a head in Brighton where I fell out with a couple of people on the streets who bad mouthed me, I turned around dropped my bags and started towards them both. As far as I was concerned, they were finished.

They left and I picked up my bags and went my way. I then started increasing my citalopram myself as it was obvious they were not working.

We talked about what I wanted out of this treatment, how it would affect me? We talked and talked so much it was educational with flashpoints and light bulb moments. I could say what I wanted and how I wanted and started to look forward to them.

We discussed the moral guilt that followed me around, the lack of identity, the not knowing what was going on. Bit by bit, I built up an understanding of why things were happening the way they did and the reaction to those.

I learnt to deal and focus on implementing change, see and control the trigger actions before the explosions, pace my life to stop such heavy daily fatigue and accept the trauma and consequences of tripping over it. Crying, an outburst of emotion is good, it is so good it should be encouraged.

For far too long, the belief of suppressing these emotions was the right thing to do and in some circumstances, it is. For the short term, you can get away with it but realistically, it does you no favours further down the road. It's not the person who deals with the traumas fault, it's sometimes the system that is not able to recognise and deal effectively with it.

My sleep hygiene routine improved and so did my sleep. My Temazepam was upped to 20mg a night and I couldn't believe the difference that made. I now slept, a process denied to me for over 6 years, 6 years of shit sleep. I realised that what I wanted to achieve and what I could achieve were far apart.

I wanted to return to the gym but with therapy, work in the house and writing, it wasn't possible and I decided to scrap the weight training for the rest of the year or until I could give the training the justice it deserved.

Continuing the trauma therapy with Gemma and along with the writing I set about finding the diaries I had written on operations. I was having difficulty remembering specifics as mentioned previously so I went scratching around the house and garage.

I found five and started reading through them, realising that I hadn't read them since I wrote them, so had no idea what was in them. What sprang to mind was the violence and continual fighting which must have seemed the norm at the time.

I soon discovered it was one operational detachment in 2007 that brought home most of the issues I now deal with. The cycle of violence and the impact of traumas were days sometimes weeks apart but a continual theme for that detachment. As I sat in the kitchen reading, I just started to breakdown and sob. This was the pivotal point, it was this, above all other detachments, that scarred me.

As the therapy progressed, so did the understanding of why I felt like I did, it was the point of remembering, it isn't that it will be forgotten but the point of they will always be remembered. It, for me, is an important lesson if you can grasp the concept.

It feels to me like the final stages of 'Saving Private Ryan' moment when the very old soldier surrounded by his family touched the gravestone of the soldier who gave his life so he could live. While my memories are not as dramatic as the film as an ex-service person, we are all joined in that understanding of those that were lost.

It doesn't even matter what war it was from; our recognition of their sacrifice is so strong; we will remember them. Those who call for stopping of Remembrance and all that about the two World Wars have little understanding of the effects that still resonate today with all those that served.

In October, Gemma asked me to identify what had changed for me in therapy. This would be a good indicator of where I was and for me to think about what the last year had achieved for me. I thought it easier to place it in bullet form.

I had accepted where I was and what had led me there. This allowed me to focus on priorities (me) which allowed me to support my other priorities, mainly Nicky and Charlie.

Accepted and learnt to control negative chatter in my head and cease going down that road if I found myself on it.

Understanding to let me be the priority and recognise my own needs. The case of look after yourself, look after others better.

I believe I had been given back the freedom to express myself and with that, I am not frightened of getting upset.

Understanding there are no victim Olympics and comparing traumas isn't a justifiable excuse of obtaining balance on your trauma. That is like comparing feet, we all have them, and they are all different.

Pacing: the art of balancing in life what you can and are capable of doing. What will require more energy, time, deliberation and rest to achieve?

Daily Schedule: a balance of life that allows you to control your days with an achievable and realistic start with not being overly concerned in moving tasks to another day.

Acknowledging the consequences of overactivity. The knock-on effect of cumulative fatigue and planning ahead for larger tasks.

Talking and writing down memories have been very cathartic and released far more memories than expected but it allowed the story to be told.

My acknowledgement of resentment towards the military and political elite.

Working at sleep hygiene and alcohol doesn't solve anything (even though it tastes nice and I love it).

In November, I started a new regime of medicines but due to the small dosage, I soon went downhill very quickly and found myself in a pit. I just wanted to run away from everything, not that I knew what I was running away from.

I was at a very low point and the realisation that I will be on meds most probably for the rest of my life. Without that control of my mind, I do find it difficult to maintain the balance between reality and paranoia which in turn sends me slightly wibble.

I also saw a psychiatrist for the first and only time and he guided me towards some different medication. Now, at the beginning of 2020, things are less busy in my head and the negativity and chatter seem to have subsided due to the change in meds.

March 2020 and the meds are still working well and I feel at peace with my world. I pace accordingly, which sees me still sleep from early evening and take a few hours in the afternoon. I haven't returned to any realistic training but a gentle dog walk after I get my lad going off to school. I hope to start again sometime in the future.

The Future

As the old saying goes, if you want something doing, do it yourself. That will become apparent on a couple of things in this last chapter.

I have attached my medical letters from one GP, a Clinical Psychologist, two Consultant Neurologists and a Consultant Psychiatrist. This is to show you how far we in the military have to go to get any kind of award or pension from the system.

It has been five years since the start of my appeal to the award of no pension or compensation from the military and seven years since the onset of my illness (April 2013). Along the way, I have suffered countless delays in receiving details which I felt ensured I didn't have the necessary details before I left the service.

I had to wait three and a half years for a service complaint to finish. I had no primary diagnosis from my medical board. The system on the medical board, I was informed after leaving, is only there for the decision of either staying or leaving the military.

It offers no guidance to the person leaving or help towards delivering a medical pension for being medically discharged and as such, bodes the question, on what does the UK Veterans agency utilise to establish their decision for a medical pension?

I received my answer from the Armed Forces Compensation Scheme (March 2020), to inform me I didn't meet the criteria for any award because they were taking the start date of my CPTSD from my seizure point in time (May 2017).

The AFCS had information on my previous counselling in Nov 2008, they have read and understood 'The girl in the white dress' and 'The face on TV' and have followed my path from 2013 onwards. But because I wasn't diagnosed earlier, I see it as an excuse for them to delay spending any money if they can get away with it.

I have also shown the letter they returned to me that says I have to wait another two years at least before I can challenge them again. You have got to laugh; you spend 28 years breaking your body and mind on wars that maybe proved rather erroneous in the future.

12 veterans have committed suicide in the last two months. I know the pain that drives you to that point of insanity or sometimes it feels like clarity.

My first point in 'if you want something doing, do it yourself' is that we as veterans are sick to death of waiting for naff all to happen and watch as our brothers and sisters in the military break so hard, the only way to stop the pain is to end your life.

One such person who is taking on this fight is Stephen Burns an ex-Royal Marine and Special Forces soldier. He was so incensed seeing his colleagues fall by the wayside, he decided to help others in need. What has flourished is a web site that has nearly 10,000 followers in less than four months from veterans, the armed services and civilian uniformed services like the police and ambulance etc. 'Op Spartan' was born.

There is no malice on this site, its purpose is for the benefit of those on there with a history of Mental Health issues that want support, the chance to air their sufferings. There is no judgement, just offerings of help, guidance and even just listening.

The point being, we all understand what others are going through, we can empathise and not let others feel less worthy. There is no victim Olympics and when life is a struggle for whatever reason, the only message is of hope and help.

This site hasn't been alive long but the belief of what it delivers has already saved others. It isn't a miracle worker, just like-minded people being there for one another when there is nowhere else to turn.

It offers motivation, guidance on courses, banter and lots of love. There are groups to join and local area representatives, information on charities and support organisations, employment opportunities, personal growth and the ability to ask 10,000 other like-minded people across the world, yep it's global, how to deal with such problems.

Secondly, me!

There is nobody more important person than yourself, that doesn't mean you only consider yourself in any situation. I've met quite enough of those selfish people along the way and the strange thing is, they will never change.

They will only look after themselves and not think twice about turning their back on others. The best thing to do is, ignore them, clear yourself away from them and enjoy the rest of your life. You have to look after yourself to provide the best for others.

At the beginning of this, whatever it was, I just wanted to return to what I knew, after I understood I wouldn't be returning, I wanted it to stop. Now I realise it's the journey that matters not the end game.

I have learned so much about myself over the last few years but especially the last two that I recognise traits in others. I'm more patient, understanding, less volatile (unless I forget my meds), but aware of my surroundings much more, kind of like being in tune with oneself.

I am still controlled by my fatigue but I have learned to pace to allow me and the family to get the best out of what I can offer rather than the push to destruction. I have to save up my body's battery for busier occasions, knowing that they will impact further down the line as punishment. My cognitive ability still falls well short of what it did and I still lose most of my short-term memory after 7-10 days.

But life is and can be rewarding, it is learning to accept and look forward to things (I can't look back). It's also changing what really is the priority in your journey of life, is it the fast flashy car, the big house, I must have this, I must have that, who are you competing against and are they even achievable?

Why is it we don't look at what we could have every day but always yearn for those items far away. Have dreams, make wishes, strive to improve and do better but keep it realistic. My realism is now the acceptance that I will never return to anything like I was previously.

I look through life sometimes through my boys' eyes, I see the joy and excitement when he discovers new things or creates great pieces of art. I listen and see more than I used to, I think it has to do with the fact that I am not stimulated in the same way by my job anymore.

I do wish I could get fit but 45 minutes of exercise comes with so much fatigue that it isn't worth the punishment.

Do what makes you happy. I love connecting with people and laughing. But I also get rewards by helping others, it is more a sense of purpose than anything else. Who knows what is around the corner, as long as when it's time to leave this life, more good than harm has been achieved in your life?

To all those still struggling out there, get help. The longer you leave it, the bigger the pop when it goes.

I am still fighting the system and will not be leaving that bone alone. And I am still trying to find my way in this new world where I am very much controlled by my comfort zones.

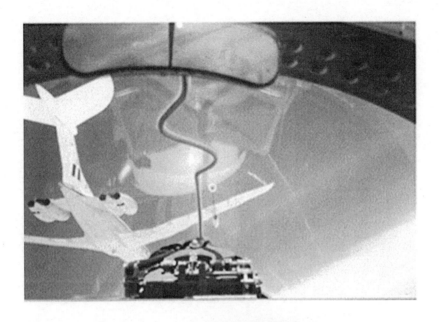

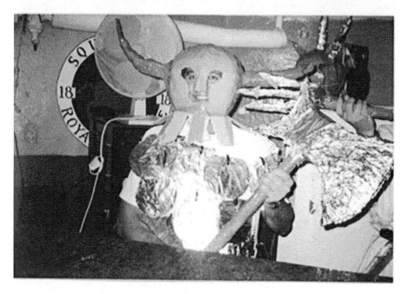

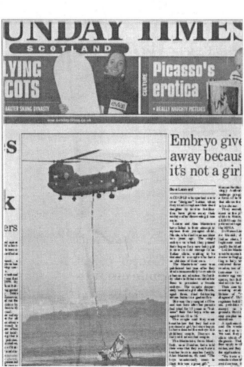

LYING
COTS
BAXTER SKIING DYNASTY
www.sunday-times.co.uk

CULTURE

Picasso's
erotica
• REALLY NAUGHTY PICTURES

Embryo give
away becaus
it's not a girl

References

1. Goethe JW. Werke. Hamburger Ausgabe. Munich, Germany: Deutscher Taschenbuch Verlag; 1998:X,234. (der Ton ist wundersam genug, als wär' er zusammengesetzt aus dem Brummen des Kreisels, dem Butteln des Wassers und dem Pfeifen eines Vogels … konnt' ich jedoch bald bemerken, daß etwas Ungewöhnliches in mir vorgehe … es schien, als wäre man an einem sehr heißen Orte, und zugleich von derselben Hitze völlig durchdrungen, so daß man sich mit demselben Element, in welchem man sich befindet, vollkommen gleich fühlt. Die Augen verlieren nichts an ihrer Stärke, noch Deutlichkeit; aber es ist doch, als wenn die Welt einen braunrötlichen Ton hätte, der den Zustand sowie die Gegenstände noch apprehensiver macht … mir schien vielmehr alles in jener Glut verschlungen zu sein … Es gehört übrigens dieser Zustand unter die am wenigsten wünschenswerten).

2. Oppenheim H. Die Traumatischen Neurosen. 2nd ed. Berlin, Germany: Hirschwald; 1892.

3. Crocq L. Les Traumatismes Psychiques de Guerre. Paris, France: Odile Jacob; 1999.

4. Crocq J. Les Névroses Traumatiques. Étude Pathogénique et Clinique. Brussels, Belgium: H. Lamertin; 1896.

5. Ellis PS. The origins of the war neuroses. Part I. J R Nav Med Serv. 1984;70:168-177.

6. Milian G. L'hypnose des batailles. Paris Med. 1915;(2 Jan):265-270.

7. Ulrich B, Ziemann B. Frontalltag im Ersten Weltkrieg. Wahn und Wirklichkeit. Frankfurt, Germany: Fischer; 1994:102-103.

8. Merskey H. Post-traumatic stress disorder and shell shock—clinical section. In: Berrios GE, Porter R, eds. A History of Clinical Psychiatry. London, UK: The Athlone Press; 1995:490-500.

9. Myers CM. Contributions to the study of shell shock. Lancet. 1915;13:316-320.

10. Brown EM. Post-traumatic stress disorder and shell shock—social section. In: Berrios GE, Porter R, eds. A History of Clinical Psychiatry. London, UK: The Athlone Press; 1995:501-508.

11. Winter D. Death's Men. Soldiers of the Great War. London, UK: Allen Lane; 1978:136.

12. Salmon TW. Care and treatment of mental diseases and war neuroses (shell shock) in the British army. Mental Hygiene. 1917;1:509-547.

13. Eissler KR. Freud und Wagner-Jauregg vor der Kommission zur Erhebung Militärischer Pflichtverletzungen. Vienna, Austria: Löcker Verlag; 1979.

14. Kaufmann F. Die planmäßige Heilung komplizierter psychogener Bewegungsstörungen bei Soldaten in einer Sitzung. In: Feldärtz Beilage Münch Med Wochenschr. 1916;63:802ff.

15. Kraepelin E. Lebenserinnerung. Berlin, Germany: Springer Verlag; 1983:189.

16. Freud S. Supplements to the Theory of Dreams. London, UK: Standard Edition; 1920;XVIII:4-5.

17. Ahrenfeldt RH. Psychiatry in the British army in the second World War. New York, NY: Columbia University Press; 1958:26.

18. Menninger WC. Psychiatry in a Troubled World. New York, NY: Macmillan; 1948.

19. Jones FD, ed. War psychiatry. Textbook of Military Medicine. Walter Reed Army Medical Center, Washington DC: Office of the Surgeon General USA; 1995.

20. Glass AJ. Neuropsychiatry in World War II. Vol II. Overseas Theaters. Washington DC: Office of the Surgeon General, Dept of the Army; 1973.

21. Kardiner A. The traumatic neuroses of war. Psychosomatic Medicine Monograph II III. Menasha, Wis: George Banta Publishing Company; 1941.

22. Kardiner A, Spiegel H. War Stress and Neurotic Illness. New York, NY: Paul B. Hoeber Inc; 1947.

23. Grinker RR, Spiegel JP. Men Under Stress. Philadelphia, Pa: Blakiston; 1945.

24. Gabriel R. Soviet Military Psychiatry: The Theory and Practice of Coping With Battle Stress. Westport, Conn: Greenwood Press; 1986:33–37.

25. Gurevich MO, Sereyskiy M Ya. Uchebnik Psikhiatrii. Moscow, Russia: Medgiz; 1946:376-377.

26. Eitinger L. Pathology of the concentration camp syndrome. Arch Gen Psychiatry. 1961;5:79-87.

27. Crocq MA, Macher JP, Barros-Beck J, Rosenberg SJ, Duval F. Post-traumatic stress disorder in World War II prisoners of war from Alsace-Lorraine who survived captivity in the USSR. In: Wilson JP, Raphael B, eds. The International Handbook of Traumatic Stress Syndromes. Stress and Coping Series. New York, NY: Plenum Press; 1992:(chap 21):253-261.

28. Belenky G (ed). Contemporary Studies in Combat Psychiatry. Westport, Conn: Greenwood Press; 1987:4.

29. Crocq L, Crocq MA, Barrois C, Belenky G, Jones FD. Low-intensity combat psychiatry casualties. In: Pichot P, Berner P, eds. Psychiatry, the State of the Art. New York, NY: Plenum Press; 1985;6:545-550.

30. American Psychiatric Association. Diagnostic and Statistical Manual of Mental Disorders, 4th ed. Washington DC: American Psychiatric Association; 1994.

31. Turner S. Place of pharmacotherapy in post-traumatic stress disorder. Lancet. 1999;354:1404-1405.